'An entertaining romp th... ations' *Time*

'As an introdu... to the subject it is an engaging read, full of thought-provoking cameos . . . this elegant... account of what the company has done for the world so... Martin Vander Weyer, *Daily Telegraph*

'John Micklethwait and Adrian Wooldridge's marvellous and concise book . . . we journey through two centuries of fascinating sociological history . . . The book is packed with entertaining vignettes of corporate history' Salil Tripathi, *Wall Street Journal*

'A lively and fast-paced history of the company, ranging widely over all forms of co-operative economic enterprise, from ancient Rome and the East India Company to Standard Oil and Microsoft' Andrew Gamble, *TLS*

'The authors show that, far from monopolising economies, the number of companies has spread and competition has increased. The authors . . . carry on at a cracking pace to give readers a good, solid introduction to a vital aspect of our lives, one that is all too easily ignored or misunderstood' *Contemporary Review*

'This "biography" asks useful questions about where the company has come from, and where it is going. *The Company* covers an impressive historical range . . . Such a broad historical canvas is excellent at putting current debates into perspective, cutting down to size the hyperbole of many corporate critics . . . Micklethwait and Wooldridge are an established and lucid writing partnership . . . by so condensing the history of the company, the authors provide a highly accessible, readable and dramatic account of corporate upheaval, crisis, and survival' Paul Morrison, *Ethical Corporation magazine*

'A swashbuckling journey through the past and into the future of the modern company' *Los Angeles Times*

John Micklethwait oversees coverage of the United States for the *Economist*. He has written articles for, among others, the *Financial Times*, the *New York Times*, the *Wall Street Journal* and the *Spectator*. He was educated at Magdalen College, Oxford. He lives in London.

Adrian Wooldridge is the *Economist*'s Washington correspondent. His writing has appeared in numerous publications, including the *New Statesman*, the *Washington Post*, *Foreign Policy*, the *Financial Times* and the *Times Literary Supplement*. He was educated at Balliol College and All Souls College, Oxford, where he received a D.Phil.

By John Micklethwait and Adrian Wooldridge

The Company: A Short History of a Revolutionary Idea

The Witch Doctors: Making Sense of the Management Gurus (*winner of a 1997* Financial Times/*Booz Allen Global Business Book Award*)

A Future Perfect: The Challenge and Hidden Promise of Globalization

Measuring the Mind: Education and Psychology in England, 1860–1990 (*Adrian Wooldridge*)

THE COMPANY

A Short History of a
Revolutionary Idea

John Micklethwait
and Adrian Wooldridge

PHOENIX

A PHOENIX PAPERBACK

First published in Great Britain in 2003
by Weidenfeld & Nicolson
This paperback edition published in 2005
by Phoenix,
an imprint of Orion Books Ltd,
Orion House, 5 Upper St Martin's Lane,
London WC2H 9EA

Originally published in the USA by Modern Library
a division of Random House, Inc.

10 9 8 7 6 5 4 3 2

A CIP catalogue record for this book
is available from the British Library.

ISBN 0 75382 040 4

Printed and bound in Great Britain by
Clays Ltd, St Ives plc

www.orionbooks.co.uk

For Richard and Jane Micklethwait
and Brian and Jill Blacker

Contents

Acknowledgments

In the best capitalist tradition, this book has been built on the backs of many underpaid and abused workers. William and Ali Mackesy, Martin Thomas, Simon Green, Leslie Hannah, Jesse Norman, Robert Miles, Mark Doyle, and Helena Douglas all helped to improve the final product, though disappointed customers should be directed to the authors alone. We would also like to thank our agent, Andrew Wylie, and our unusually tolerant editor at Random House, Scott Moyers. Our editor at *The Economist*, Bill Emmott, has once again been extremely supportive, and we would also like to apologize to those poor souls – Ann Wroe, John Parker, Zanny Minton-Beddoes, Rachel Horwood, Venetia Longin, and Lucy Tallon – who have had to put up with us at close quarters. However, the main burden has yet again been shouldered, sometimes silently, by our wives and children. Our liability to them is indeed unlimited.

Introduction: Utopia Limited

On the evening of October 7, 1893, a new operetta opened to a packed house in London's West End. William S. Gilbert and Arthur Sullivan were the titans of Victorian popular culture, with amateur musical societies putting on performances of *The Pirates of Penzance* and *The Gondoliers* from Brighton to Bombay. Richard D'Oyly Carte had built a special theater at the Savoy just for their works. Adding to the air of expectation, the two writers had quarreled a few years earlier, partly because Sullivan aimed higher than mere comic opera, and it had looked as if their long collaboration was coming to an end. Now they were back.

One of the themes of *Utopia Limited, or The Flowers of Progress*, was not an obvious rib-tickler: the limited-liability joint-stock company. That night's operetta made fun of the idea that companies were sweeping all before them, enriching investors as they went. An English company promoter named Mr. Goldbury arrives in the exotic South Sea Island of Utopia and sets about turning the inhabitants into companies. Even babies issue company prospectuses. At one point in the final act, the King of Utopia demands, 'And do I understand you that Great Britain/Upon this Joint Stock principle is governed?' And Mr. Goldbury replies, 'We haven't come to that, exactly – but/We're tending rapidly in that direction/The date's not distant.' Soon afterward, the Utopians join in one of the most improbable choruses ever set to music: 'All hail, astonishing

Fact!/All hail, Invention new/The Joint Stock Company's Act/The Act of Sixty-Two!'

For all its barbs, *Utopia Limited* sounded a triumphant note. It was a celebration of yet another quirky Victorian invention that had changed the world. The new companies, set free by 'the Act of 1862' and by its imitators in other countries, were speeding the first great age of globalization. They were luring millions of people off the land, changing the way that people ate, worked, and played. They were erecting the first towering offices in Manhattan and despoiling the Belgian Congo. They were battling with labor unions and challenging politicians. 'This is a government of the people, by the people and for the people no longer,' warned President Rutherford B. Hayes: 'It is a government of corporations, by corporations and for corporations.' The year before the curtain went up on *Utopia Limited*, the Ohio Supreme Court ruled that Standard Oil had created a monopoly. Even in Britain, which had nothing to match John D. Rockefeller's oil empire, many of the bourgeois gentlemen chuckling knowingly in the boxes at the D'Oyly Carte theater owed their fortunes to the new device; and the stalls probably squeezed in at least one impoverished aristocrat who had blown his inheritance gambling on American railroad stocks.

Nowadays, the influence of this unsettling organization is even more pervasive. Hegel predicted that the basic unit of modern society would be the state, Marx that it would be the commune, Lenin and Hitler that it would be the political party. Before that, a succession of saints and sages claimed the same for the parish church, the feudal manor, and the monarchy. The big contention of this small book is that they have all been proved wrong. The most important organization in the world is the company: the basis of the prosperity of the West and the best hope for the future of the rest of the world. Indeed, for most of us, the company's only real rival for our time and energy is the one that is taken for granted – the family. (Meanwhile, in a nice reversal of fortune, the world's best-known family, the British monarchy, on whose whims and favors many of the earliest English joint-stock companies depended, now refers to itself as 'the firm.')

That does not mean that the role of the company has been appreciated, least of all by political historians. The great Companies Acts of the mid-nineteenth century get barely a sentence in most recent biographies of William Gladstone, one of their political champions; the intellectual godfather of the modern company, Robert Lowe, is more remembered for his work on education and his grumpy opposition to universal suffrage. The relevant volume of the *New Oxford History of England* that covers 1846 to 1886 does not find room to discuss the invention of the company in its 720 pages.[1]

In fact, the history of the company is an extraordinary tale. What often began as a state-sponsored charity has sprawled into all sorts of fields, reconfiguring geography, warfare, the arts, science, and, sadly, the language. Companies have proved enormously powerful not just because they improve productivity, but also because they possess most of the legal rights of a human being, without the attendant disadvantages of biology: they are not condemned to die of old age and they can create progeny pretty much at will. This privilege of immortality, not to mention the protection that the artificial corporate form has afforded various venal people down the ages, has often infuriated the rest of society – particularly governments. Hence, there has been a lengthy series of somewhat bad-tempered laws trying to tamper with the concession – from the Statute of Mortmain, which Edward I issued in 1279 to stem the flow of assets being transferred beyond his feudal writ to the 'dead hand' of corporate bodies (particularly monasteries), to the 2002 Sarbanes-Oxley Act, through which Congress tried to make bosses more accountable for the sins of 'their' companies.

There are two ways to define a company. The first is merely as an organization engaged in business: this definition, as we shall see, includes everything from informal Assyrian trading arrangements to modern leveraged buyouts. The second is more specific: the limited-liability joint-stock company is a distinct legal entity (so distinct, in fact, that its shareholders can sue it), endowed by government with certain collective rights and responsibilities. This was the institution that the Utopians' 'Astonishing Fact,' the Companies Act of 1862, unleashed, and which is still spreading around the world, conquering such obstinate refuseniks as the Chinese Communist Party and the partners of Goldman Sachs.

Though this is primarily a book about the joint-stock company, it unapologetically strays into broader territory. From the beginning of economic life, businesspeople have looked for ways to share the risks and rewards of their activities. One of the fundamental ideas of medieval law was that 'bodies corporate' – towns, universities, guilds – had a life beyond that of their members. In the sixteenth and seventeenth centuries, European monarchs created chartered companies to pursue their dreams of imperial expansion. One of these, the East India Company, wound up ruling India with a private army of 260,000 native troops (twice the size of the British army). Another, the Virginia Company, helped to introduce the revolutionary concept of democracy to the American colonies, to the fury of James I, who called it 'a seminary for a seditious parliament.'[2] Yet another, John Law's Mississippi Company, wrecked the economy of France, Europe's richest country in the eighteenth century.

Yet William Gilbert was right to think that something fundamental changed in nineteenth-century Britain. The most powerful economic power of the day finally brought together the three big ideas behind the modern company: that it could be an 'artificial person,' with the same ability to do business as a real person; that it could issue tradable shares to any number of investors; and that those investors could have limited liability (so they could lose only the money they had committed to the firm). Just as important, the Victorians changed the point of companies. It was no longer necessary to seek special sanction from parliament to set one up or to limit its business to a specific worthy aim (like building a railway between two cities); now it was possible to set up general-purpose corporations at the drop of a hat. All that was necessary was for seven people ('If possible, all Peers and Baronets,' Goldbury mischievously advised the Utopians) to sign a memorandum of association for the company to be registered and for it to use the word 'limited' to warn creditors that they would have no recourse to the company's owners.

The Companies Acts, which were rapidly copied in other countries, unleashed entrepreneurs to raise money, safe in the knowledge that investors could lose only what they had put in. They also gave birth to an organization that soon seemed to acquire a life of its own, swiftly mutating from one shape to another, with government usually unable to restrain it. Nowadays, nobody finds it odd that, a century after its foundation, the Minnesota Mining and Manufacturing Company makes Post-it notes, or that the world's biggest mobile-phone company, Nokia, used to be in the paper business.

The Victorians also gave us many of the most profound arguments that swirl around companies. Nowadays it is assumed that the causes of capitalism and companies are inseparable. Yet many of the earliest critics of the joint-stock company and the 'subsidy' of limited liability were economic liberals, taking their cue from Adam Smith, who had derided them as antiquated and inefficient. One noted Victorian thinker, A. V. Dicey, fretted that the company would become the harbinger of a new age of collectivism: 'one trade after another' would pass from the 'management of private persons into the hands of corporate bodies created by the state.'[3] (Karl Marx gave a grudging welcome to companies for much the same reason.)

For the company's early critics, it was not just a question of allowing investors to repudiate responsibility for their debts; many Victorian liberals also worried whether professional managers could be trusted to act in the interests of the owner shareholders. They had a point: the potential conflict of interest between the 'principals' who own companies and their 'agents,' who run them, which was later dubbed the agency problem, has dogged the history of the company, from the mills of Lancashire to software start-ups in Palo Alto, with shareholders repeatedly trying to find ways to make managers' interests the same as their own (most recently with share options) and managers usually wriggling out of them. John Stuart Mill settled his own doubts on this score only by wearily concluding that for new capital-hungry businesses, like railways, the only alternative to the joint-stock system was direct state control.

Even after the Companies Acts, Victorians were still prey to the traditional cultural prejudices against these soulless institutions. The *Morning Post* ran a xenophobic campaign against the railway companies on the grounds that they were exporting British jobs. At the same time, American populists denounced the very same companies on the grounds that the British were trying to recolonize the country by stealth. In Anthony Trollope's *The Way We Live Now* (1875), a company, supposed to build a great railway linking Mexico and the United States, is hijacked by an unscrupulous continental financier, Augustus Melmotte, and his American partner, Hamilton K. Fisker. Its board, consisting of know-nothing aristocrats and unscrupulous politicians, meets for a perfunctory fifteen minutes. ('There was not one of them then present who had not after some fashion been given to understand that his fortune was to be made, not by the construction of the railway, but by the floating of the railway shares.')[4] And the whole enterprise predictably results in a speculative crash.

In America, where the influence of companies was greatest, the howls against 'the malefactors of great wealth' reached a crescendo at the beginning of the twentieth century. Yet no sooner had society reined in the robber barons than it discovered that a still less accountable villain had seized control of the company: the faceless manager. The rise and fall of the juggernauts of corporate America forms a large part of our story. Of course, not everybody worked for them – but it sure felt that way. Until 1975, the big American corporation was the model against which all other sorts of company were measured. Yet, since then, Company Man, too, has been chased out. Companies have become flatter, less hierarchical organizations.

Throughout the twentieth century, the company jostled with the state that spawned it. European and Asian governments tried to run companies of their own – and failed spectacularly. Many on the Left would argue that companies tried to set up governments of their own – and succeeded equally spectacularly. Meanwhile, the ways that companies have subtly influenced our lives have multiplied. It was a company – Lever Brothers – that introduced us to the concept of 'BO.' ('It was not enough to produce satisfactory soap,' Joseph Schumpeter once observed. 'It was also necessary to induce people to wash.')[5] It is a company – McDonald's – that is credited with teaching the Chinese how to queue.[6]

Three themes stand out in our story. First, the company's past is often more dramatic than its present. Modern business books may have macho titles such as *Barbarians at the Gate* and *Only the Paranoid Survive*, but early businessmen took risks with their lives as well as their fortunes. Send a fleet to the Spice Islands at the beginning of the seventeenth century, and you might be lucky if a third of the men came back alive. This was a time when competitive advantage meant blowing your opponents out of the water, when marketing meant supplying an English rose for the sultan's harem (a London merchant of 'honorable parentage' selflessly offered his daughter), and when your suppliers might put your head on a stick.[7]

The second point is to some extent a correlation of the first. In general, companies have become more ethical: more honest, more humane, more socially responsible. The early history of companies was often one of imperialism and speculation, of appalling rip-offs and even massacres. People who now protest about the new evil of global commerce plainly have not read much about slavery or opium. People who talk in terrified tones about the unprecedented skulduggery at WorldCom seem to have forgotten about the South Sea Bubble. Those who fear the unparalleled might of Bill Gates could do with a little reading on J. P. Morgan. Today, the number of private-sector companies that a country boasts – the United States had 5½ million corporations in 2001, North Korea, as far as we can tell, none – is a better guide to its status than the number of battleships it can muster. It is also not a bad guide to its political freedom.

This leads to the third point. The company has been one of the West's great competitive advantages. Of course, the West's success owes much to technological prowess and liberal values.

But Lowe and Gladstone ushered in an organization that has been uniquely effective in rendering human effort productive. The idea that the company itself was an enabling technology is something that liberal thinkers once understood instinctively. 'The limited liability corporation is the greatest single discovery of modern times,' proclaimed Nicholas Murray Butler, one of the great sages of the Progressive Era; 'even steam and electricity would be reduced to comparative impotence without it.'

Economists have elaborated on why such institutions are crucial to economic development.[8] Companies increase the pool of capital available for productive investment. They allow investors to spread their risk by purchasing small and easily marketable shares in several enterprises. And they provide a way of imposing effective management structures on large organizations.[9] Of course, companies can ossify, but the fact that investors can simply put their money elsewhere is a powerful rejuvenator.

A cluster of competing companies makes for a remarkably innovative economy. Nowadays, you only have to look at Silicon Valley to grasp this point. But in the mid-nineteenth century, the effect of Western governments delegating key decisions about which ideas to back to independent firms was revolutionary.[10] Rather than being trapped in government monopolies, capital began to search for the most efficient and flexible companies; and rather than being limited by family partnerships, it came together in bigger and bigger conglomerations. By contrast, civilizations that once outstripped the West yet failed to develop private-sector companies – notably China and the Islamic world – fell farther and farther behind. It cannot be just coincidence that Asia's most conspicuous economic success is also the country that most obviously embraced companies – Japan.

This book is an attempt to chart the rise of this remarkable institution. But we have also taken the liberty to spend a little time puzzling about its future. At first sight, that future should be assured. Nation-states are on the defensive. Churches are struggling to find recruits. Trade unions are a mere shadow of their former selves. But companies are going from strength to strength. Most people in the West now work for companies, which also produce the bulk of the world's products.[11] Any young Napoleon who yearns for the scent of global conquest would be better off joining a company than running for political office or joining the army.

Yet, the company is much less powerful than it seems. Although the influence of companies as a species has never been more widespread, the clout of individual big companies has arguably declined. The much-vaunted idea that companies are now bigger than mere governments is, as we shall see, statistically fraudulent. Big companies are giving way to small ones, so much so, in fact, that an old question is now more pressing: What is the point of companies?

That question was most succinctly answered back in 1937 by Ronald Coase, a young British economist. In an article called 'The Nature of the Firm,' he argued that the main reason why a company exists (as opposed to individual buyers and sellers making ad hoc deals at every stage of production) is because it minimizes the transaction costs of coordinating a particular economic activity. Bring all the people in-house, and you reduce the costs of 'negotiating and concluding a separate contract for each exchange transaction.'

But the gains from reducing transaction costs that companies deliver have to be balanced against 'hierarchy costs' – the costs of central managers ignoring dispersed information. In the nineteenth century, the gains to be had from integrating mass production with mass distribution were enormous – as Alfred Chandler, the doyen of business historians, puts it, the 'visible hand of managerial direction' replaced 'the invisible hand of market mechanisms.' In the twenty-first century, technology and globalization are helping to reduce barriers to entry – and thus helping to unbundle the corporate package. At the touch of a button, a mere journalist can get access to more information than a corporate giant could amass a decade ago. The fashion nowadays is for virtual companies – for airlines that do not own their own planes, for banks that do not have branches, for the invisible hand to claw back ground from the visible one.

That should not imply that the company is beginning a slow, inevitable decline. Despite the seductive charm of frictionless capitalism, most people seem to like being in companies. (We should admit that through luck, absence of opportunity, laziness, and, especially, the charity of others, we have both remained at the same organization for most of our working lives.) The economic argument has also deepened since Coase, with some economists preferring to look at the firm as a network of contracts and others seeing it as a bundle of organizational capabilities. But the basic questions being asked by modern investors, managers, and workers – What does this company do? Why do I work here? Will it make money? – are worth remembering as we head back into the past.

1 *Merchants and Monopolists*
3000 B.C. — A.D. 1500

Before the modern company came of age in the mid-nineteenth century, it had an incredibly protracted and often highly irresponsible youth. The merchants and marauders, imperialists and speculators, who dominated business life for so many centuries might not have formed fully fledged companies as we know them, but they nevertheless created powerful organizations that changed commercial life.

As long ago as 3000 B.C., Mesopotamia boasted business arrangements that went beyond simple barter. Sumerian families who traded along the Euphrates and Tigris rivers developed contracts that tried to rationalize property ownership.[1] The temple functioned as both bank and state overseer. The Assyrians (2000–1800 B.C.), a group one normally associates with biblical savagery, took this farther. One document shows an Assyrian ruler formally sharing power with the elders, the town, and the merchants (or *karum*, named after the word for quay, where they sat).[2] There was even a partnership agreement. Under the terms of one such contract, some fourteen investors put twenty-six pieces of gold into a fund run by a merchant called Amur Ishtar, who himself added four. The fund was to last four years, and the merchant was to collect a third of the profits – terms not dissimilar to a modern venture-capital fund.[3]

The Phoenicians and later the Athenians took this sort of capitalism to sea with them, spreading similar organizations around the Mediterranean. The expense and time involved in maritime commerce made some type of formal arrangement even more necessary than its land-based equivalent. So did the ever-present danger, for investors and creditors alike, that a sea captain would simply disappear. (Homer, the first of a long line of storytellers to distrust traders of all sorts, denounces merchants from Tyre for being duplicitous.)

The Athenian model stood out because it relied on the rule of law rather than the whim of kings, and because it was unusually open to outsiders. A banker and ship owner named Pasion, who died in 370 B.C. as one of the city's richest men, originally arrived as a barbarian slave. Yet, Athenian businesses remained small beer, typically mustering no more than a handful of people; even shield factories, the largest-known businesses, seldom employed more than one hundred slaves.[4]

The *societates* of Rome, particularly those organized by tax-farming *publicani*, were slightly more ambitious affairs. To begin with, collecting taxes was entrusted to individual Roman knights; but as the Empire grew, the levies became more than any one noble could guarantee, and by the Second Punic War (218–202 B.C.), they began to form companies – *societates* – in which each partner had a share. These firms also found a role as the commercial arm of conquest, grinding out shields and swords for the legions.[5] Lower down the social scale, craftsmen and merchants gathered together to form guilds (*collegia* or *corpora*) that elected their own managers and were supposed to be licensed.[6]

William Blackstone, the great eighteenth-century jurist, claimed that the honor of inventing companies 'belongs entirely to the Romans.'[7] They certainly created some of the fundamental concepts of corporate law, particularly the idea that an association of people could have a collective identity that was separate from its human components. They linked companies to the *familia*, the basic unit of society. The partners – or *socii* – left most of the managerial decisions to a *magister*, who in turn ran the business, administered the field agents, and kept *tabulae accepti et expensi*. The firms also had some form of limited liability. On the other hand, the *societates* were still relatively flimsy things, 'mere groups of individuals,' as one historian puts it.[8] Most tax-farming contracts were for short terms. And most wealth was still concentrated in agriculture and private estates.[9]

When Rome crumbled, the focus of commercial life moved eastward – to India, and particularly to China and the Islamic world. The prophet Mohammed (569–632) was a trader. If the religion that he founded banned usury, it nevertheless encouraged responsible moneymaking: while Christian businessmen often found their work at odds with their creed, Muslim merchants like Sinbad could be heroes. To this moral advantage, they could add a couple of geographic ones. First, they sat between West and East. Thousands of Muslim merchants had reached China before Marco Polo appeared. And, second, many Arabs lived in barren places with only rudimentary agriculture. In Mohammed's Mecca, there was precious little for a young man to do other than become a trader.

The Chinese, meanwhile, opened up a huge technological lead over the West. Within a decade of William the Conqueror dispatching Harold at the Battle of Hastings (1066), Chinese factories were producing 125,000 tons of iron a year – a figure Europe would not match for seven hundred years. The Chinese pioneered paper money. During his travels in China in 1275 to 1292, Marco Polo marveled at trading junks large enough to provide sixty merchants with their own cabins. Even by the time that Vasco da Gama made it round the Cape of Good Hope to East Africa in 1497, his much-better-dressed hosts, accustomed to China's huge ships, wondered how he could have put to sea in such puny craft.

The debate about why the Chinese and Arabs lost their economic lead to the West is a huge one. Suffice to say here that their relative failure to develop companies was part of their broader geographic and cultural shortcomings. Islamic law allowed for a form of flexible trading partnership, the *muqarada*, which let investors and traders pool their capital. But, for the most part, the law relied on oral testimony rather than written contracts. And the inheritance law rooted in the Koran rigidly divided up a dead partner's estate between countless family members (as opposed to the European system, which usually allowed partners to nominate a single heir). This tended to prevent Muslim firms from growing to a size where they needed to raise capital from outsiders.[10]

In China's case, the idea of permanent private-sector businesses was undermined both by culture and by state interference. Chinese merchants evolved elaborate partnerships: by the fourteenth century, there were a number of different categories of investor and merchant. But these partnerships seldom lasted much longer than a few voyages.

Meanwhile, many of the big 'companies' that did emerge in China relied on the state. Hereditary bureaucrats ran state monopolies in many industries, including porcelain. These businesses often enjoyed huge economies of scale – until the eighteenth century, Chinese factories were far more impressive than anything the West could offer. Yet, the state monopolies suffered from the opposite problem from the businesses of merchants: they were not temporary enough. The very vastness of China counted against them. As we shall see, European state monopolies were also inefficient and corrupt, but they were at least kept on their toes and prevented from becoming so bureaucratic by having to compete with state monopolies from other countries.

In the end, China's determination to look inward proved fatal. Arguably the zenith of Chinese economic imperialism came in the early fifteenth century, when the Ming emperor Yung Lo, who ascended the throne in 1403, built a fleet of huge treasure ships, which he dispatched around Asia. But after Yung's death in 1424, his son stopped the treasure ships and gave their most famous seafarer, Zheng He, a landlubber's job. Crucially, he also ordered all mercantilist exploration to stop. Later emperors rebuilt trade relations with other Asian countries, but their ambitions were limited. In 1793, the Chinese emperor sent a message to Britain's George III: 'As your ambassador can see, we possess all things. . . . There is therefore no need to import the manufactures of outside barbarians in exchange for our own produce.' This was an unfortunate attitude, for by then China's merchants faced a formidable new form of business organization.

THE RIALTO EFFECT

Two sorts of medieval organization picked up where the Romans had left off: the merchant empires of Italy, and the state-chartered corporations and guilds of northern Europe.

Maritime firms appeared in Italian towns such as Amalfi and Venice from the ninth century onward.[11] The earliest version, modeled on the Muslim *muqarada*, was usually created to finance and manage a single voyage (which might last for several months). This arrangement was particularly attractive to the stay-at-home capitalist, allowing him to diversify his risks over a number of cargoes while avoiding the trouble of going to sea himself. These partnerships gradually became more complex, financing multiple voyages, adding foreign partners, and devising new ownership structures. For instance, Venetian merchants formed consortia to lease galleys from the state. Each voyage was financed by issuing twenty-four shares among the partners.[12]

In the twelfth century, a slightly different form of organization emerged in Florence and other inland towns: the *compagnia*. These began as family firms, operating on the principle of joint liability: all partners were jointly liable to the value of their worldly goods ('to their cuff links,' as all-too-liable investing 'names' at Lloyds of London would later put it). Given that the punishment for bankruptcy could be imprisonment or even servitude, it was vital that all the members of the organization should trust each other absolutely. The word *compagnia* is a compound of two Latin words (*cum* and *panis*) meaning 'breaking bread together.'

Like their Venetian equivalents, the *compagnie* became more sophisticated as time went by, trying to attract investment from outside the family circle. Perhaps as early as 1340, they introduced double-entry bookkeeping, largely to keep their foreign offices honest. A Genoese merchant would record money sent to his agent in Bruges as 'paid' in his accounts, while the latter put down the amount as 'received.' And rather than sending coins, the bigger merchants began to trust each other with letters of exchange – a business that Italian banks would dominate.

Indeed, the *compagnie* were closely intertwined with the *banchi* (named after the *banco*, or bench, behind which Italian money lenders used to sit). In the *Inferno* (1314), Dante gleefully sent usurers to the seventh circle of hell to be tortured by a rain of fire, and in many cities bankers were forbidden, along with prostitutes, from receiving communion. Many *banchi* were little more than pawnbrokers, charging outrageous rates of interest (often above 40 percent a year). But the *grossi banchi* were sophisticated, well-capitalized international banks, able to settle bills of exchange in different cities. They lured rich investors away from real estate toward bank deposits (which were much more mobile in the event of a political crisis). And they helped to finance not just voyages and companies but even kingdoms. When Edward III of England defaulted in 1339 he eventually brought down Florence's two most important banks, the Bardi and the Peruzzi. By 1423, Florence's addiction to warfare left it with a public debt six times the size of its annual tax revenues (roughly double the proportion that the United States ran up in the early 1990s).[13]

The Medici bank, which eventually spawned four popes and two queens of France, and provided much of the capital for the Renaissance, was set up in 1397 by Giovanni di Bicci de' Medici. The family's great advantage was that it secured the papacy's business: until 1434, more than half its revenues came from its Roman 'branch,' which followed the pope around on his travels. To get around the papal ban on Christians receiving interest, bankers like the Medici were often paid in foreign currencies (with hidden premiums) or with licenses or with goods, thus sucking them into other businesses. The Medici diversified, via the wool trade, into clothmaking, and, notably, a monopoly on alum, a chemical fixative indispensable in dyeing textiles.

As the Medici expanded – they opened branches in ten cities – they minimized their exposure to losses by organizing each branch as a separate partnership. They also devised profit-sharing arrangements to give all the partners a strong incentive to maximize returns.[14] They even tried to ban their managers from lending to princes. But, in the end, their commercial power relied mostly on their personal supervision. Under Cosimo de' Medici (1389–1464), that supervision was tough. The bank even managed to prevent the elevation of one young cleric to a bishopric until his father (a cardinal, as it happens) had paid off both their debts. But after Cosimo died, his descendants allowed the bank to slip downhill. The Wars of the Roses left it with bad debts in London, and the firm's interest in the wool trade dragged it into lending to the crown. In 1478, it lost the papal banking business. By 1494, when the family was expelled from Florence, their bank had already closed many of its branches.

DATINI'S DATABASE

How similar were these organizations to modern companies? Let us pause for a moment to look at a fourteenth-century business.[15] Francesco di Marco Datini was born in relatively humble circumstances in the Tuscan town of Prato in about 1335 and orphaned soon thereafter. As a young man, he set out for Avignon, where he probably worked as an apprentice before striking out on his own. Despite doing business under the motto 'For God and Profit,' Datini's first venture was in arms-dealing, though he soon branched into more innocent partnerships, involving shops, textiles, and jewelry. He returned to Prato in 1382, driven out of Avignon by a papal squabble with the Florentines. By the end of the century, his *compagnie* dealt in everything from slaves to pilgrims' robes in nine cities. Datini had also – slightly nervously – become a banker. When he died ten years later, the childless merchant bequeathed almost all his money (some 100,000 florins), his house, and all his papers to a foundation for the poor of Prato.

'The Merchant of Prato' was something of a control freak:

Datini recorded everything and told his managers to do the same. The business that emerges from the 150,000 letters, 500 ledgers, and 300 partnership agreements that he left behind often seems remarkably modern. The near-daily letters from the *capo* to his various *fattori* around Europe asking for news and numbers, their replying boasts and excuses, his reprimands ('You cannot see a crow in a bowl full of milk'), read a little like e-mail. There is the persistent need for lawyers, for the right papers, for up-to-date accounts. Promotions are awarded, employees trained, disgruntled partners appeased; all the while, Datini's wife frets about her husband working too hard. Even his hard-won profits seem meagerly modern: all this hard labor eked out a mere 9 percent margin.

Yet, if many of the incidental noises of business are familiar, the environment is not. This was the time of the Black Death, of the revolt of the Florentine weavers against the guilds, of periodic bursts of violent religious fervor that often targeted moneymakers. As his biographer, Iris Origo, points out, Datini 'lived in daily dread of war, pestilence, famine and insurrection, in daily expectation of bad news. He believed neither in the stability of government, nor the honesty of any man. . . . It was these fears that caused him to distribute his fortune in as many places as possible, never trusting too much to any partner, always prepared to cut his losses and begin again.'[16]

Despite his obsession with running everything, Datini was a fervent supporter of *compagnie*. 'I am one of those who hold that two partners or brothers who are united in the same trade and behave as they should, will make greater profits than each of them would separately.'[17] Since partners were liable for each other's debts, most people still stuck to kith and kin (Datini chose Tuscans). For much the same reason, the terms of partnerships were usually only two years, though these could be renewed.

His will dictated that his shares in his companies should be wound up within five years of his death. If he had had children, Datini's 'company' might have lasted longer. But it was plainly in any independent merchant's interest to keep things as loose and flexible as possible: permanence was the prerogative of the state. So it is unsurprising that the state played a big role in the creation of corporations. This was an area in which northern Europe led the way.

CORPORATIONS AND GUILDS

Northern Europe, it should be stressed quickly, did not lack for trading companies any more than Italy lacked for guilds. Northern merchants copied many of the arrangements that the Italians pioneered.[18] Some of the businesses were huge undertakings. For instance, Germany's *magna societas*, a combination of three family firms based in Ravensburg, had subsidiaries in cities as far apart as Barcelona, Genoa, and Paris, sent representatives to fairs all around the Continent, and lasted for 150 years, ending up with eighty partners and a capital of 120,000 florins. All the same, the most important contribution from the north were guilds and chartered companies.

In the early Middle Ages, jurists, elaborating on Roman and canon law, slowly began to recognize the existence of 'corporate persons': loose associations of people who wished to be treated as collective entities. These 'corporate persons' included towns, universities, and religious communities, as well as guilds of merchants and tradesmen. Such associations honeycombed medieval society, providing security and fellowship in a forbidding world. They also provided a means of transmitting traditions – not to mention considerable wealth – to future generations. The Corporation of London, which dates back to the twelfth century, still owns a quarter of the land in the City of London, as well as three private schools, four markets, and Hampstead Heath. Many of the companies that vie to be called the world's oldest date back to this period. The one with the best claim, if you ignore ostensibly noncommercial entities like monasteries, is the Aberdeen Harbour Board, which was set up in 1136. (The oldest existing private-sector company in Europe is probably Stora Enso of Sweden, whose direct ancestor, a copper mine, began trading in 1288 and was issued with a royal charter in 1347.)

The immortal status of these bodies clearly worried the crown. They circumvented feudal fees by never dying, never coming of age, and never getting married. In 1279, Edward I issued the Statute of Mortmain, which was aimed at limiting the amount of land passing to corporate bodies, particularly the church. Unauthorized transfers without the monarch's permission could result in forfeiture.

None of this stopped corporate bodies growing. For much of the Middle Ages, guilds were the most important form of business organization. A guild (based on the Saxon verb *gildan*, to pay) typically enjoyed a monopoly of the trade within a city's walls in return for substantial monetary donations to the sovereign. Its officers set standards for quality, trained members, appointed notaries and brokers, administered charitable work, built magnificent guildhalls that survive till this day, and imposed punishments. In London, a man who served a seven-year apprenticeship in one of the liveried guilds could become a freeman, which brought exemption from conscription and also allowed him to establish his business within the walls of the City of London.

The guilds were often more like trade unions than companies, more interested in protecting their members' interests than in pursuing economic innovation. Indeed, once their medieval heyday was behind them, they often descended into Luddism. (In 1707, members of the boatmen's guild in Germany ambushed the French inventor Denis Papin and destroyed the world's first steamboat: steam power was not used in shipping until a century later.)

Guilds were closely related to 'regulated companies': associations of independent merchants who were granted monopolies of trade with particular foreign markets. Like guilds, these bodies trained new members through apprenticeships, and conducted periodic peer reviews (as they might be called today) to screen out less successful members. But they also sometimes operated as consortia – the merchants clubbing together to negotiate better prices for raw materials and transport (in much the same way that the Venetian galley lessors did). The most successful of the regulated companies was the Staple of London, which was founded in 1248 to control wool exports.[19] In 1357, the Staple acquired the right to collect customs on wool exports in return for helping to finance Edward III's French wars. In 1466, Henry VI granted the Staple authority over Calais (including the right to collect customs on woolen imports bound for the Continent) in return for similar finan-cial help.

So even if the crown remained nervous about ceding powers to bodies corporate, it was still crucial to their development. The state offered security, and the promise of a guaranteed market was as alluring to groups of medieval merchants as it is to defense contractors nowadays. Over the next few centuries the story of the company would be bound up with the overseas ambitions of the emerging nation-states of northern Europe.

2   *Imperialists and Speculators*
1500–1750

The sixteenth and seventeenth centuries saw the emergence of some of the most remarkable business organizations the world has seen: 'chartered companies' that bore the names of almost every part of the known world ('East India,' 'Muscovy,' 'Hudson's Bay,' 'Africa,' 'Levant,' 'Virginia,' 'Massachusetts') and even of bits that were too obscure to bear names ('The Company of Distant Parts'). These companies were complex entities. In 1700, the British East India Company employed over 350 people in its head office, more than many modern multinationals. They were also remarkably long-lasting. The East India Company lasted for 274 years. The Hudson's Bay Company, which was founded in 1670, is still with us, making it the world's oldest surviving multinational.

Chartered companies represented a combined effort by governments and merchants to grab the riches of the new worlds opened up by Columbus (1451–1506), Magellan (1480–1521), and Vasco da Gama (1469–1524). All of them were the lucky recipients of royal charters that gave them exclusive rights to trade with this or that bit of the world. They thus bestraddled the public and private sectors. Sometimes, the monarch insisted on a share in the firm himself, as Colbert (1619–1683) did on the French king's behalf when he set up his country's East Indies company in 1664. But, in general, northern European governments, led by the English and Dutch, preferred to operate through independent companies.

These chartered companies also drew on two other ideas from the Middle Ages. The first was the idea of shares that could be sold on the open market. The idea of offering shares in enterprises dates back at least to the thirteenth century. Across Europe, you could buy shares in mines and ships.[1] In Toulouse, mills were divided into shares that their holders could sell like real estate. But the naval capitalism of the sixteenth and seventeenth centuries dramatically expanded the idea, bringing stock exchanges in its wake. The other idea, which had occasionally surfaced before, was limited liability. Colonization was so risky that the only way to raise large sums of money from investors was to protect them.

The first chartered joint-stock company was the Muscovy Company, which was finally given its charter in 1555. Two decades earlier, a group of London merchants had dispatched a fleet in a predictably disastrous attempt to find a northern passage to the East Indies; one boat got as far as Archangel – and attracted the notice of the czar, Ivan IV, who was keen to increase trade with England. Under the Muscovy charter, eventually won by a consortium including the famous navigator Sebastian Cabot (1483–1557), the Company was given a temporary monopoly over trade routes to the Russian port (and also encouraged to continue the search for a northeast passage). The company was able to raise enough money to finance the long journey to Russia by selling tradable shares. The Muscovy Company faded from view after about 1630, but it spawned a host of imitators seeking other monopolies.

Some of them looked west. Richard Hakluyt (1552–1616), an eminent geographer, was responsible for whipping up interest in America – and for persuading Elizabeth I to grant charters to several groups of investors. His *Discourse on Western Planting* (1584), which he presented to the queen, was arguably one of the first company prospectuses.[2] Colonizing America, he argued, would be 'a great bridle to the Indies of the King of Spain,' delivering fishing fleets that 'we may arrest at our pleasure'; it would advance 'the enlargement of the gospel of Christ' by converting the heathen; and, of course, it would yield up not just North American treasure but also 'all the commodities of Europe, Africa and Asia.'[3] The Virginia Company duly raised funds from seven-hundred-odd Elizabethan 'adventurers,' including Sir Francis Bacon – and produced, in return, no profits.

The main prizes were to the east. The risks of investing in voyages to the spiceries of Indonesia would be akin to the risks of investing in space exploration today. Indeed, the quarter century before the creation of the two main East Indies companies showed why charters, shares, and limited liability were so necessary. In 1582, having failed to find a northeast passage, the London merchants pinned their hopes on one Edward Fenton, who duly headed out into the Atlantic and unveiled a new plan to his crew: to capture the island of St. Helena and 'there to be proclaimed king.'[4] In 1591, the merchants backed the far more competent James Lancaster: three years, six weeks, and two days later, his ship limped back home with a paltry cargo, having lost all but 25 of his 198 men to disease and storms. In 1595, the Dutch chose a former spy, Cornelis de Houtman: he bombarded Bantam, a vital Javan port, executed a bunch of locals, poisoned one of his own captains, and returned home with two-thirds of his crew gone. His backers were saved by the inflation in spice prices, which meant that the miserable amount he brought back covered their costs. But that was not something they could count on: the market for spices remained small and was easy to swamp with just a couple of deliveries.[5]

It was hardly surprising that the Dutch merchants decided that state-sponsored collusion was preferable to this. The monopoly that they eventually secured from the state in 1602 – the Dutch East India Company, alternatively known as the VOC (for Vereenigde Oost-Indische Compagnie) or the Seventeen (after its seventeen-strong board) – became the model for all chartered firms. Whereas the English East India Company initially treated each voyage as a separate venture, with different shareholders, the VOC made all the voyages part of a twenty-one-year venture (something the English imitated a decade later). The VOC's charter also explicitly told investors that they had limited liability. Dutch investors were the first to trade their shares at a regular stock exchange, founded in 1611, just around the corner from the VOC's office. All the Amsterdam hub needed to prove its capitalistic credentials was a market crash, which duly arrived with tulip mania in 1636–1637.

If the Dutch set the fashion for stock-market speculation at home, they also set the tone for competitive imperialism abroad. The VOC's first voyage had the simple instructions: 'Attack the Spanish and Portuguese wherever you find them.' Within forty years, the VOC had established itself as the dominant force in the Moluccan Spice Islands, driving the Portuguese away and forcing the English to concentrate on India. The Dutch founded an Atlantic equivalent to the VOC, the Westindische Compagnie, in 1621. But they remained fixated by the spiceries. In 1667, they famously swapped their small North American trading center, New Amsterdam (better known nowadays as Manhattan), for the nutmeg-rich spice island of Run.

It would be wrong to claim that the great chartered companies were the commercial norm for the next two centuries. Most business life continued in smaller enterprises, typically partnerships, where all the employees could be gathered in one family home. Fernand Braudel claims that the biggest bank in Paris on the eve of the revolution employed only thirty people.[6] At various points in this period, there were brief spasms of enthusiasm for the joint-stock concept among smaller businessmen (there was one splurge in London in the 1690s).

Still, it was the big chartered companies that hogged the limelight. And it was thanks to their abuses that, as late as 1800, many reformers saw the joint-stock company as dangerous and old-fashioned. The main evidence for the prosecution came from the most remarkable company of the period, the English East India Company, and from its most remarkable financial scandal – the frothy combination of the South Sea Bubble and the collapse of the Mississippi Company.

THE HONORABLE COMPANY

The East India Company was more than just a modern company in embryo. 'The grandest society of merchants in the Universe' possessed an army, ruled a vast tract of the world, created one of the world's greatest civil services, built much of London's docklands, and even provided comfortable perches for the likes of James Mill and Thomas Love Peacock.[7]

It all began on September 24, 1599, when a group of eighty merchants and adventurers, including veterans of the Levant Company and a few of Francis Drake's crew, met at the Founders Hall in the City of London. Under the chairmanship of the lord mayor, Sir Stephen Soane, they agreed to petition Elizabeth I to set up a company to trade with the East Indies. They also elected fifteen directors. At first, things went well: Elizabeth gave her provisional approval. But her Privy Council stalled over the necessary paperwork. Politicians worried that the voyage would derail a peace treaty with Spain, and there was a tug of war over who would command the venture. The court wanted the aristocratic Sir Edward Michelbourne, who had himself been lobbying for an East Indies monopoly. The merchants said they would prefer 'a man of their own quality' rather than 'a gentleman,' and they wanted James Lancaster as their commander.

The merchants won. On December 31, 1600, 'the Governor and Company of Merchants trading to the East Indies,' a group of 218 men, was granted a charter, giving them a monopoly for fifteen years over trade 'to the East Indies, the countries and ports of Asia and Africa, and to and from all the islands' ports, towns, and places of Asia, Africa and America, or any of them beyond the Cape of Good Hope and the Straits of Magellan.' Two months later, Lancaster set sail with five ships.

In September 1603, Lancaster returned in triumph. Despite the usual disasters (a quarter of his men were dead by the time he reached the Cape), he had set up a factory in Bantam and brought back all five ships and five hundred tons of pepper. Unfortunately, there was a hitch: the monarch himself – now James I – had just acquired a shipload of pepper, and insisted that his should be sold first. The 218 members of the Company were told that for every £250 they had each invested, they now had to subscribe another £200 to pay for the next voyage.

The young company faced fierce opposition from the Dutch and the Portuguese. Michelbourne caused all manner of problems: he persuaded James I to allow him to go on a voyage of discovery and then plundered many of the young company's customers. The Company also had a hard time satisfying the demands of its foreign clients. The Sultan of Achin wanted an English rose for his harem, for example. The greedy merchants were willing to oblige, and even found a girl 'of excellent parts for music, her needle and good discourse,' but they eventually ran up against James I's opposition.[8]

None of this took the wind out of the young company's sails. The early voyages proved remarkably profitable. The tenth voyage, in 1611, for example, earned a return of 148 percent on its shareholders' capital of £46,092.[9] The Company probed new markets extending from the Red Sea to the East Indian Archipelago. In 1612, it had the confidence to move from financing one voyage at a time to financing several voyages at once. The Company's first joint-stock offering in 1613–1616 raised £418,000; its second (1617–1622) raised a colossal £1.6 million.[10] By 1620, it boasted thirty to forty large and heavily armed ships, which traveled in convoys of twelve or more vessels.[11]

The Company soon established a routine of sixteen-month-long voyages. On the outward leg, scheduled in late winter to take advantage of favorable winds, its most important cargo was silver, normally bought abroad by the Company's network of continental agents (mercantilist philosophy objected to exporting the metal directly from England). The cargo also included other things that were easy to trade: lead, tin, mercury, corals, ivory, armor, swords, satins, and broadcloths.[12] In India, most of this was exchanged for cotton textiles, which was then traded in the Spice Islands for pepper, cloves, and nutmeg. Sometimes an excursion to China, Japan, or the Philippines added silk, indigo, sugar, coffee, and tea. But the normal route was back via India, where part of the spice cargo was traded for tea, which found a ready market in Europe.[13]

All this required sophisticated administration. Most of the Company's predecessors, such as the Levant Company, had been little more than regulatory bodies, supervising the activities of the syndicates that did the real business of raising capital and trading on their own accounts. The East Indies merchants created a two-tier structure. The General Court included all the shareholders with voting rights: many of these were bigwigs from court and parliament. The day-to-day management was entrusted to the Court of Directors, twenty-four men all elected by the General Court. The governor and his deputy, assisted by a growing number of accountants, clerks, and cashiers, worked through seven committees specializ-ing in accounting, buying, correspondence, shipping, finance, warehousing, and private trade. The Court of Directors also supervised the overseas network of resident 'factors' who managed the local trading posts, or factories.

This whole elaborate structure depended on the quality of these factors. They were prey to all sorts of dangers, from war-lords, diseases, and the climate, and to constant temptations, not least the temptation to enrich themselves rather than their employers. The Company made a point of selecting the sons of its bigger shareholders to fill the jobs. It encouraged loyalty by paying generous salaries and referring to the firm as a 'family.' It inculcated diligence by encouraging them to go to church daily, and came down hard on drunkenness, gambling, and extrava-gance. The head office scrutinized the factors' performance against statistical averages, and asked their friends and relatives to submit confidential appraisals of their abilities. It also made factors post bonds indemnify-ing the Company against losses resulting from misconduct.

FOR KING AND COUNTRY

This all sounds organized enough. Yet, the plain fact is that the Company nearly died in the mid-seventeenth century. At home, it was almost undone by politics, particularly by the English civil war (1642–1649) and Oliver Cromwell, who was more sympathetic to free trade. Overseas, it was effectively driven out of the Spice Islands by the brutal VOC. In January 1657, the General Court, in an emergency session, agreed to sell the island of Run and its factories in Surat and Bantam for a mere £14,000. But Cromwell relented. On October 19, the Company was reborn with a new charter, establishing it on a more permanent basis: the merchants of London promptly subscribed some £786,000. The new Company, making a virtue out of necessity, decided to focus more on India – and prospered mightily. Peace, a succession of successful voyages, and a dramatic expansion of the Company's powers (Charles II allowed the directors to acquire land and declare war) all led to huge profits.

By the late seventeenth century the Company was a well-organized monopoly, providing some £20,000 in customs duties to the crown. But it was still a state monopoly – and one mired in politics. Fellow merchants resented its power and ambitious courtiers plotted to appropriate a share of its profits. Mercantilists accused it of draining away the country's precious silver. Nonshareholders resented the spoils enjoyed by their more fortunate countrymen. (In 1680, the Company paid a 50 percent dividend and a single share sold for as much as £300.)[14] Even disinterested critics had questions. Should a single monopoly account for nearly half of Britain's trade? Should British businessmen govern overseas territories? Should a company possess a private army?

There was hardly a time when someone wasn't raising one of these pesky questions, or meddling in the Company's affairs. The Whig revolutionaries who deposed James II in 1688 promoted a rival company (which eventually merged with the existing one in 1708–1709). In 1700, the government banned the sale of Asian silks and fancy cottons in England, forcing the

Company to find another profitable line in the form of Chinese tea.

The Company also became deeply involved in Indian politics. For a long time, it vacillated between cooperating with the locals and imposing direct control. The balance gradually slipped toward direct control, as the locals proved incompetent and the factors spotted a regular income in tax farming. All the same, by 1700, there were no more than fifteen hundred Britons in India, most of them in fortified encampments such as Calcutta's Fort William, and they also had to 'share' India with the French Compagnie des Indes, which was in a similar quandary.

The decisive figure in the Company's evolution was Clive of India (1725–1774). Robert Clive, a hotheaded clerk who had already tried to commit suicide twice, was one of the few Company men to escape when the French seized Madras in 1746. In 1751, he led an audacious raid with eight hundred men to capture the fortress town of Arcot; more remarkably, he then fought off a fifty-day siege by a far greater French and Indian force. After a brief stint in England, he was tempted back to Madras in 1756, recapturing Calcutta and then vanquishing the Nawab of Bengal at the Battle of Plassey. That and a subsequent English victory over the Moghul emperor at Buxar in 1764 cemented the Company's control over Bengal, paved the way for its other acquisitions, both hostile and friendly, and relegated the French to mere onlookers.

'Commerce steels the nerves of war/Heals the havoc Rapine makes,/And new strength from Conquest takes,' gushed the poet laureate, William Whitehead. But many Britons were resentful. Clive was dogged by questions about the despoiling of Bengal. The Company's employees had become so synonymous with ostentatious wealth that they gave the English language a new word: nabobs or nobs. 'What is England now? A sink of

Indian wealth,' fumed Horace Walpole.

In 1767, the Company bought off parliamentary opposition by promising the crown £400,000 a year in return for undisturbed possession of Bengal. It had miscalculated: in 1772, it was forced to ask for a gigantic loan of £1 million in order to avert bankruptcy. The loan came with a stinging parliamentary report by the Burgoyne Committee, the revelation of more malpractice, and, at last, a successful attempt at suicide by Clive. But his death did little to clear the smell of scandal. Warren Hastings, the first official governor-general of India, from 1773 to 1784, and the architect of tighter British control over the Moghul Empire, was impeached by parliament, though a lengthy trial eventually vindicated him.

Nevertheless, it was under Clive and Hastings that the Company transformed itself into a form of government – 'an empire within an empire,' as one director admitted. As tax revenues replaced commercial profits, a proliferation of boards, councils, and committees sprang up in both London and India. Its outward-bound ships were more likely to be loaded with soldiers and guns than they were with broadcloth. Even in China and the Far East, where the Company's remit was more strictly commercial, it faced increasing competition from nimbler private entrepreneurs. The rise of both the Royal Navy and maritime insurance had reduced the risks of foreign trade, in effect eroding the raison d'être for the chartered monopolies.[15]

Unsurprisingly, critics argued that this ever-more political body should be nationalized. The 1773 decision by parliament to give the Company a monopoly over tea in America helped provoke the Boston Tea Party, and with it the American Revolution. In 1784, William Pitt's India Act imposed a new government Board of Control, though it left the directors in charge of its day-to-day business. The Company was also caught up in the debate over slavery. In the 1790s, Elizabeth Heyrick launched the first consumer boycott, urging her fellow citizens in Leicester to stop buying 'blood-stained' sugar from the West Indies; the Company was eventually forced to get its sugar from slaveless sugar producers in Bengal.

In the nineteenth century, the government used the renewal of the Company's license, which occurred every twenty years, to bring it under even tighter control. In 1813, the government abolished its monopoly of trade. In 1833, it deprived it of its right to trade altogether, turning it into a sort of governing corporation. In 1853, with the introduction of competitive examinations for its staff, the Company lost its remaining powers of patronage. When the Indian mutiny broke out in 1857, the Honorable Company became the scapegoat for the uprising (not altogether unfairly: one revisionist historian has argued that the dispute was not about imperialism or even forcing Hindus to use pigskin cartridges, but about the Company's stifling lock on job opportunities for ambitious locals).[16] The Company's army passed to the crown; its navy was disbanded; and, when its charter expired on June 1, 1874, this extraordinary organization passed away quietly, with less fanfare than a regional railway bankruptcy.

JOHN LAW AND THE GOD MAMMON

Early joint-stock companies were instruments of rampant financial speculation as well as economic imperialism. In the early eighteenth century, the governments of France and Britain used two chartered companies – the Mississippi Company in France and the South Sea Company in England – to restructure the vast debts that they had accumulated during the wars of 1689 to 1714. Their aim was to reduce the cost of servicing the public debt by converting government annuities, which paid fixed interest, into lower-yielding shares. The result was the biggest financial bubble in history, bigger even than the bubble of the 1920s in the United States.

The man who set the whole disaster in motion was John Law (1671–1729).[17] The son of a wealthy Scot, Law spent an irresponsible youth in London indulging his passions for women, gambling, and mathematics, but he was eventually forced to flee to Amsterdam after killing a rival in a duel. There he managed to amass a huge fortune through financial speculation. In 1704, he returned to Scotland with hopes of a royal pardon and ambitious schemes for introducing paper money. The royal pardon was not forthcoming, and he took his schemes back to the Continent.

His big break came in 1715, when a rakish young regent, Philippe, the Duke of Orléans, succeeded Louis XIV. The two men knew each other from Paris's gambling dens. In May 1716, Law persuaded the duke to allow him to set up a Banque Générale, charged with issuing banknotes. Law's plan was to rescue France from its rampant inflation, shortages of coins and unstable currency, by introducing paper money. The regent deposited a million livres with the new bank, ordered French tax collectors to remit payments to the treasury in banknotes, and invited the public to pay taxes in notes. In December 1718, with assets exceeding 10 million livres, the bank was transformed into the Banque Royale.

With the French money supply under his control, Law then bid for the trading concession belonging to the Compagnie d'Occident, which he rechristened the Mississippi Company, converting a chunk of French national debt into shares in the firm. Soon afterward, the Mississippi Company acquired a succession of other overseas trading monopolies – and threw in the

Royal Mint for good measure. One monopoly now controlled the entire colonial trade of the most powerful nation on earth.

Law issued a large number of shares in his businesses, but kept speculative fever high by announcing generous dividends and allowing existing shareholders to buy yet more shares at a preferential rate. His boldest move came in 1719 when he offered to convert the entire national debt from annuities into company shares; he also offered a huge sum for the right to take over royal tax collection. He financed all this by issuing large numbers of shares.

The result was mass frenzy. Mobs of investors, from aristocrats to valets, besieged Law's offices. By one account, some 200,000 investors, hailing from Venice, Genoa, Germany, and England, as well as the French provinces, converged on Paris. Law allowed investors to buy shares in installments, paying 10 percent of the purchase price each month; at the same time, he provided loans from the Banque Royale on the security of shares. Between December 25, 1718, and April 20, 1720, the value of the banknotes issued by the Banque Royale rose from 18 million livres to 2.6 billion livres. The price of single shares in the Mississippi Company reached 10,000 livres. At the height of the bubble, Law sold call options, allowing investors to pay a deposit of 1,000 livres for the right to buy a 10,000-livres share within the next six months. 'It is inconceivable what wealth there is in France now,' mused one observer. 'Everybody speaks in millions. I don't understand it at all. But I see clearly that the God Mammon reigns an absolute monarch in Paris.'[18]

Law's control of both the central bank and the stock market allowed him to avoid the tedious question of what his company actually did. Law liked to tell aristocrats that the Mississippi Company provided a great opportunity for missionary work in the colonies: he even brought specimen Indians to Paris in his ships.[19] But the Mississippi Company's real activities in North America, spiritual or anthropologi-cal, were fairly meager. Louisiana – the one bit of America that France controlled – was relatively poor and backward. As Niall Ferguson notes, Law was reduced to conscripting orphans, criminals, and prostitutes to populate his Promised Land.

The bubble inevitably burst. In early 1720, a growing tide of investors began to abandon the Mississippi Company (many shifting their investments to the new bull market in London). Using his powers as controller general, Law tried desperately to stem the outflow of capital. The value of his shares and ban-knotes continued to tumble regardless, and he was forced to abolish the paper currency and close the Banque. In December 1720, false passport in hand, he fled to Brussels, leaving France in chaos.

THE SOUTH SEA BUBBLE AND THE CAROUSEL OF FOOLS

The drama of the South Sea Company did not quite reach the heights of the Mississippi Company. The British had several advantages, including the fact that the Whig-controlled Bank of England, created in 1694, remained outside the control of the Tory-backed South Sea Company; indeed, they were often at war.[20] And the South Sea officials were never able to use exchange-control regulations when the price of their shares began to fall. Yet the overall scam was the same.

The South Sea Company was founded in 1711 with a monop-oly of trade with Spanish America. By 1719, war with Spain was strangling this business, so its directors decided to focus instead on the market for public debt. The architect of the scheme was John Blunt, the son of a prosperous Baptist shoemaker and a man with a genius for turning the language of the Bible into advertising jingles. ('The greatest thing in the world is referred to you,' he said at one point. 'All the money in Europe will center amongst you. All the nations of the earth will bring you tribute.')[21] His company's directors, mostly men of wealth and reputation, included Edward Gibbon's grandfather and namesake.[22]

On January 21, 1720, a parliamentary announcement proclaimed that the Company would take over the entire British national debt, absorbing annuities with a capital value of around £30 million. Even before the measure was enacted on April 7, the South Sea Company's share price rose rapidly from £128 in January to £187 in mid-February. The subscriptions were filled in hours. The share price reached £950 by the beginning of July, with foreign investors joining the stampede. Even without the example of Law, the timing was propitious. There was widespread belief that public debt needed to be retired as quickly as possible. The country was in a euphoric mood buoyed by military successes against the French.[23] There had also been a boomlet in the creation of small new companies, many of them set up to exploit government-granted patents, which in turn had spawned a new sort of person who traded their shares – the stockjobbers who frequented the coffeehouses around Exchange Alley.

The South Sea directors worked hard at exciting this market, using the same sorts of devices as John Law, and paying particular attention to the new financial press. Quotations for South Sea stocks even appeared in local papers like the *Plymouth Weekly Journal*. William Hogarth mocked the speculative frenzy with his cartoon *The Carousel of Fools*. Unfortunately, the directors did their job too well. A flood of proposals for new companies engulfed Exchange Alley, prompting the South Sea directors to persuade their political allies to pass the ironically named Bubble Act of June 11, 1720. This made it extremely difficult to set up a new joint-stock company, thus reducing the number of enterprises that would compete with the South Sea Company for capital.

The act, which was not repealed for a century, was a disaster for the evolution of the Company. It was also pointless, since the collapse of the South Sea Company later that summer punctured the market anyway. By August, a desperate credit crunch hit London. By October, the Company's share price was back to £170. Eventually, the government effectively nationalized the Company, leaving the investors with large losses, but saving most of the financial system. [24] All the same, the Chancellor of the Exchequer and several directors of the Company were consigned to the Tower of London. And what the prime minister, Sir Robert Walpole, called 'the never to be forgotten or forgiven South Sea scheme' still damned the name of joint-stock companies of all sorts.[25]

A BODY WITHOUT A SOUL

The damage done to companies by these shenanigans was immense. These organizations had raised hackles from the very beginning. Sir Edward Coke (1552–1634), for example, had complained that 'they cannot commit treason, nor be outlawed or excommunicated, for they have no souls.' Two centuries later, the lord chancellor, Edward Thurlow (1731–1806), echoed his words: 'Corporations have neither bodies to be punished, nor souls to be condemned, they therefore do as they like.'[26]

Were they really that bad? Both the South Sea and Mississippi companies bilked thousands of investors of their money. Worse still, chartered companies often found their hands covered in blood. They pioneered slavery (which we will cover in more detail in the next chapter). In India, the East India Company intimidated its local rivals, particularly the country's native indigo growers. As one anonymous pamphlet put it in 1773, 'Indians tortured to disclose their treasure; cities, towns and villages ransacked, jaghires and provinces purloined: these were the 'delights' and 'religions' of the Directors and their servants.'[27] Clive based his defense partly on that refuge of all multinational scoundrels: that India was a barbaric, uncivilized place, so anything went there.

On the other hand, in America, chartered companies sometimes played a more enlightened role. Sir Edwin Sandys (1561–1629), the treasurer of the Virginia Company, first earned James I's wrath by making a speech in the British House of Commons questioning the legitimacy of any government not based on a mutual contract between ruler and ruled. In 1619, the Virginia Company effectively introduced representative democracy into the colonies, authorizing a General Assembly in which members elected the company's officers.[28] John Winthrop (1588–1649) took Massachusetts down the same road in 1630 when the General Court of the Massachusetts Company transformed itself into a commonwealth, redefining 'freemen' from stockholders in a commercial venture to citizens of a state.[29] Roughly put, the General Courts evolved into increasingly rebellious state legislatures.

Economic liberals produced a different array of charges. Adam Smith (1723–1790), who was obsessed with the East India Company's abuses in Bengal, had two basic complaints. First, he disliked the fact that chartered companies possessed monopolies (albeit ones that were being diluted, even as he scribbled away, by both licensed and clandestine competition). For him, the chartered companies were 'either burdensome or useless' and they 'either mismanaged or confined' trade.[30] Second, he thought that joint-stock companies were inherently less efficient than sole traders. In particular, he worried about the 'agency' problem: hired managers would not bring the same 'anxious vigilance' to their firms' interests as owner-managers. 'Negligence and profusion, therefore must always prevail. . . .'

Yet, it is possible to defend the chartered corporations a little on both these counts. First, as we have seen already, chartered monopolies did make some sense, given the enormous risks of trading with the other side of the world.[31] And whatever the merits of mercantilism, the northern European model, in which the state subcontracted imperialism to companies, proved much more successful than the southern European model (notably in Spain), where the crown directly sponsored economic imperialism.

As for Smith's second charge – that the chartered firms were less efficient than owner-managed companies – this, too, is open to dispute. For all its faults, the East India Company demonstrated that when information was scarce and trust at a premium, a company could be more efficient than individual agents trading in the market. The Company's network of trusted factors compiled information that could never be gathered by any private businessman rooted in one local market (its ledger book took two hundred pages just to list the goods purchased in one voyage). And it used this knowledge to build a complex trading system to its own advantage.[32]

The East India Company's other great step forward was to provide a cradle for Company Man. Its administrators were collectively known as 'civil servants' long before government employees thought of calling themselves by the same name. During the impeachment of Warren Hastings, Edmund Burke described the rule of the company as 'a government of writing and a government of record.'[33] James Mill, who combined his job at the Company with writing the *Elements of Political Economy* (1821), explained that 'the business, though laborious enough, is to me highly interesting. It is the very essence of the internal government of sixty million people with which I deal.'

Like all bureaucracies, this one had its inefficiencies. Mill's son, John Stuart Mill (1806–1873), who wrote much of *System of Logic* (1843) and *Principles of Political Economy* (1848) during office hours, found 'office duties an actual rest from the other mental occupations which I have carried on simultaneously with them.'[34] Thomas Love Peacock, who was actually one of the Company's more dedicated employees, wrote a satirical poem on the time-wasting inherent in much office life.

> From ten to eleven, at a breakfast for seven;
> From eleven to noon, to begin twas too soon;
> From twelve to one, asked 'what's to be done?'
> From one to two, found nothing to do;
> From two to three began to foresee
> That from three to four would be a damned bore.

Any organization that provides a rest home for poets and philosophers cannot be entirely bad. All the same, something had to be done to reinvigorate the idea of the company. That is the subject of our next chapter.

3   A Prolonged and Painful Birth
1750–1862

In 1733, an Irish satirist called Samuel Madden (1687–1765) published an early venture in science fiction. The pamphlet, entitled *Memoirs of the Twentieth Century*, predicted that two giant companies would dominate the world in that far-off time: the Royal Fishery and the Plantation Company (to be founded by Frederick I and George III respectively).[1] As a prophecy of the influence of companies two centuries away, this was oddly prescient – all the more so because Madden was polemicizing against a declining economic organization.

Set beside partnerships and various forms of unincorporated companies, incorporated joint-stock companies (i.e., ones recognized by state statute) fared badly for the next century. The British and the French treated them with suspicion. 'They are behind the times,' thundered one governor of Pennsylvania, 'they belong to an age that is past.'[2] New companies were chartered, of course; but the process of doing so was cumbersome. It was not until a combination of legal and economic changes from the 1820s onward that the modern company began to take shape.[3]

SLAVERS AND INDUSTRIALISTS

In Britain, the prejudice against joint-stock companies created by the South Sea Bubble was later reinforced by scandals involving both the Charitable Corporation and the York Building

Company. As we have already noted, the ironically named South Sea Bubble Act survived the scandal. It required every joint-stock company to possess a charter from parliament – something that involved huge costs in terms of money, time, and uncertainty. Most British businessmen preferred other sorts of organizations, such as partnerships and various unincorporated companies (partnerships that tried to mimic some of the qualities of companies by making their shares freely transferable and doing something to limit the liability of sleeping partners who were not directly involved in the business).[4]

There were several frenzies of joint-stock company creation – most notably to build canals. Between 1758 and 1803, 165 canal acts were submitted to parliament. The Napoleonic Wars produced another flurry: in January 1808, forty-two companies were formed, an unusual number of them related to the business of helping the British to get drunk. In the first quarter of 1824, 250 private bills were filed at parliament to set up companies, many of them in the insurance business.[5] But it was plainly a cumbersome, sporadic process.

Symptomatically, the two most dynamic and controversial parts of the British economy – the slave trade and the growing industrial sector – both preferred partnerships (and occasionally joint-venture associations) to joint-stock companies. By the eighteenth century, the Royal African Company, like all the other chartered companies set up for slavery, was a financial failure.[6] As Britain's slave trade moved from London to Bristol and Liverpool, the RAC began to give way to partnerships of wealthy traders. In 1750, the government officially opened up the British slave trade, leaving it under the control of a club, the Company of Merchants Trading to Africa, which took over the RAC's ports and forts.

The newly deregulated business prospered as never before,

the slavers soon rivaling the East India nabobs in their wealth. In 1757, the leading contributor to a huge government loan was Richard Oswald, a Glaswegian merchant, political go-between, and slaver who owned property on both sides of the Atlantic (including a share in Bence Island, off Sierra Leone, where his partnership set up a golf course, with kilted slaves as caddies). By 1798, some 150 ships a year were leaving Liverpool for Africa. In the final decade of the eighteenth century, when one prime minister guessed that three-quarters of the country's overseas earnings were coming from slave-related business, the British shipped some 400,000 slaves.

Yet, the Bristol and Liverpool slavers did their business through small partnerships, just as their rivals did in Bordeaux, Nantes, and Rhode Island. Six or seven merchants, often related to each other, financed most slave voyages. Isaac Hobhouse, a Bristol merchant who financed forty-four voyages between 1722 and 1747, had just seven partners, two of them his brothers. Over in Rhode Island, John Brown brought his brothers into the business. Indeed, slavery in both Europe and America increasingly became, as Hugh Thomas writes in his history of the trade, 'a thing of families: the Montaudoins, the Nairacs, the Foäches, the Cunliffes, the Leylands, the Hobhouses, the de Wolfs, the Browns.'[7] Even these empires remained fairly small: the biggest, the Montaudoins in Nantes, financed no more than eighty voyages. Typically, the partners were jacks-of-all-trades, with slaves being only one of the commodities the families handled.

Joint-stock companies were also unpopular with early industrialists. To people like Richard Arkwright, Abraham Darby, and Josiah Wedgwood, partnerships made more sense than joint-stock companies. The amount of capital required for manufacturing ventures was not large. A group of Lancashire mill owners could raise enough capital to build a new factory. As for limited liability, that was viewed, to the extent that it was considered at all, as a weakness rather than a strength, because it would lower the commitment of the partner-owners. 'It is impossible for a mill at any distance to be managed unless it is under the direction of a partner or superintendent who has an interest in the success of the business,' argued Sir Robert Peel, Britain's richest industrialist in the 1820s and father of the eponymous prime minister.[8] In Elizabeth Gas-kell's *North and South*, published in the 1850s, the 'master' of the mill, Mr. Thornton, deals directly with his workers. His house is in the shadow of the mill: hence his mother's famous comment about 'the continual murmur of the work people' disturbing her no more than 'the humming of a hive of bees.'

For the most part, it was remarkable how far the industrialists, like the slavers, were able to keep the ownership and management of their businesses within a small circle. This was certainly true of Boulton & Watt. Matthew Boulton (1728–1809) inherited a small family hardware business in Birmingham. By 1769, through a mixture of graft, intellectual curiosity, and shrewd marriage, he was already, in Josiah Wedgwood's judgment, 'the first manufacturer in England.' His Soho Manufactory, which employed eight hundred workers to turn out metal boxes, buttons, chains, and sword hilts, was so famous that guided tours had to be arranged. (People were equally amazed by Boulton's centrally heated mansion, Soho House.) Then, in 1774, he went into partnership with James Watt (1736–1819), the Scottish pioneer of the steam engine, whose first partner-backer had just gone bust following a poor mining investment. On March 8, 1776, they demonstrated Watt's machine in Birmingham: it rapidly became indispensable to the coal industry and then cotton mills. By the time they retired in 1800, handing the business over to their sons, Boulton and Watt counted among the richest people in the country, and Britain was producing 15 million tons of coal a year, about five times the total production of continental Europe.

Again, like the slavers, the industrialists relied on some degree of government sanction. One of Boulton & Watt's first actions was to obtain patents from parliament – to the fury of their competitors, who complained that the patents were so broad that they could just as well have been for 'a nice and warm water closet.' But Boulton & Watt remained firmly a private partnership, run by two men – to the cost of William Murdock, another prodigiously gifted inventor employed by them. Had he been a partner, he might have earned them even more money: in the 1780s, forty years before the Stockton-Darlington Railway, Murdock drew up a plan for a steam locomotive, which Watt dismissed immediately with 'small hopes that a wheel carriage would ever become useful.'[9]

AN AMERICAN ALTERNATIVE

In Britain, the marginal position of joint-stock companies could easily be blamed on the South Sea Company's abuses. In newly independent America, by contrast, companies had been responsible for the country's very existence.

The early American states used chartered corporations, endowed with special monopoly rights, to build some of the vital infrastructure of the new country – universities (like America's oldest corporation, Harvard University, chartered in 1636), banks, churches, canals, municipalities, and roads. The first business corporation was probably the New London Society for Trade and Commerce, a Connecticut trading company chartered in May 1732. Symptomatically, the Connecticut General Assembly revoked its corporate charter within a year, in February 1733. Such shenanigans help explain why business corporations were exceedingly rare before the late eighteenth century; indeed, there were no business corporations whatsoever in the South until 1781.[10]

After independence, things sped up a little. The Bank of North America was the first wholly American corporation, chartered by the Continental Congress in 1781. The Society for Establishing Useful Manufactures of New Jersey, chartered in 1791, was the first to be formed after the ratification of the American Constitution. In 1795, North Carolina passed an act that allowed canal companies to incorporate, without getting specific permission. Four years later, Massachusetts gave its water-supply companies the same option. By 1800, there were 335 business corporations in the country, nearly two-thirds of them in New England. Transport companies (including canals, toll bridges, and turnpikes) were the most common, followed by banking. Manufacturing and trading companies made up only 4 percent of the total.[11]

Most of these companies had monopolies, but governments were notoriously fickle, rewriting charters on a whim. In 1792, for instance, the General Court altered the Massachusetts Bank's charter for purely political reasons. Twenty years later, an attorney successfully argued that 'the notion of a contract between the government and a corporation' was 'too fanciful to need any observation.' Businessmen could never assume that incorporation granted lasting rights.[12] (Conversely, even the most powerful politicians couldn't rescue a bad idea: the Potomac Company, created in 1785 to make the Potomac River navigable, boasted George Washington as its president and Thomas Jefferson as a director. It still failed.)[13]

Wall Street's slow development did not help matters. The

curbside markets of New York, which gradually replaced Philadelphia as the main exchange, were notoriously volatile, partly because they depended so heavily on flighty British capital. They also focused on government bonds. Wall Street did not trade a corporate stock until 1798, when the New York Insurance Company came to market. America's early tycoons, such as John Jacob Astor (1763–1848) and Stephen Girard (1750–1831), were players on the exchange, buying great chunks of government debt. But they ran their own businesses as private partnerships – as did America's slavers, such as the Browns, and early industrialists such as Eli Whitney (1765–1825).

SETTING THE COMPANY FREE

The fact that business on both sides of the Atlantic was still rooted in partnerships did not make partnerships perfect. Unlimited liability restricted a firm's ability to raise capital. The untimely death of a key partner or even an heir often killed the firm with it: Mr. Dombey's problems in *Dombey and Son* (1848), Charles Dickens's great novel about a family firm, stem from the death of his son. Partnerships were prey to scoundrels of all kinds. Dombey entrusts the day-to-day running of his business to James Carker, and does not discover how badly he is doing until Carker runs off with Dombey's wife. Partnerships were fragile creations. Businesspeople stuck to them because they didn't like bringing the state into their private affairs.

In the first half of the nineteenth century, the state began to step back. It did so first in America – though because of the federal system, it was a much more piecemeal and convoluted affair than in Britain. There were three prompts for change. The most important was the railroad, which we will discuss later. The second was legal. In a ruling about the status of Dartmouth

College in 1819, the Supreme Court found that corporations of all sorts possessed private rights, so states could not rewrite their charters capriciously.

The last prompt was political. Concerned that their states were losing potential business, legislatures, particularly in New England, slowly began to loosen their control over companies. In 1830, the Massachusetts state legislature decided that companies did not need to be engaged in public works to be awarded the privilege of limited liability. In 1837, Connecticut went further and allowed firms in most lines of business to become incorporated without special legislative enactment.

This competition between the states was arguably the first instance of a phenomenon that would later be dubbed 'a race to the bottom,' with local politicians offering greater freedom to companies to keep their business (just as they would much later dangle tax incentives in front of car companies to build factories in their states). All the same, it is worth noting that the states gave away these privileges grudgingly, often ignoring the Dartmouth College ruling and often hedging in 'their' companies with restrictions, both financial and social. The Pennsylvania Coke and Iron Company, chartered in 1831, was compelled to produce five hundred tons of iron within three years using only bituminous coal or anthracite in the process.[14] A bank charter in New Jersey required the company to help local fisheries. New York limited corporations to $2 million in capital until 1881 and to $5 million until 1890. In 1848, Pennsylvania's General Manufacturing Act set a twenty-year limit on manufacturing corporations. As late as 1903, almost half the states limited the duration of corporate charters to between twenty and fifty years. Throughout the nineteenth century, legislatures revoked charters when the corporation wasn't deemed to be fulfilling its responsibilities.

THE *MIDDLEMARCH* EFFECT

There was also a fierce debate in Europe about whether to sever the Gordian knot between companies and public works. As the memory of John Law faded, France loosened its rules, albeit fitfully. Alongside the huge, established *sociétés anonymes*, which had to be authorized by the government, a new form of business was made available to entrepreneurs in 1807 – a partnership with transferable shares, the *société en commandite par actions*. This granted limited liability to its sleeping (inactive) partners and only needed to be registered.[15] Another pioneer was Sweden, which gave legal recognition to joint-stock firms as early as 1848.

All the same, only a legal pedant would dispute the boast in *Utopia Limited*: that Victorian Britain gave birth to the modern company. Throughout the first half of the nineteenth century, the leaders of the world's most important economy labored to free up its commercial laws. Parliament made the currency convertible to gold (1819), relaxed the restrictive Combination labor laws (1824), opening the East India Company's markets to competition (1834), and eventually repealed the protectionist Corn Laws (1846).

They also began to tackle the issue of company law. In 1825, parliament finally repealed the vexatious Bubble Act. Reformers called for the statutory recognition of unincorporated companies, but conservative judges were skeptical. Lord Eldon, for example, maintained that it was an offense against the common law to try to act as a corporation without a private act of parliament or a royal charter.[16] Despite attempts to speed up the process of obtaining charters, it could still be expensive – one estimate put the cost at £402 – and fraught with political risk.[17]

The crucial change was the railways, and their demands for large agglomerations of capital. In 1830, George Stephenson's Rocket began steaming down the Liverpool-Manchester line, the world's first regular passenger railway. By 1840, two thousand miles of track, the bare bones of a national network, had been built – all by chartered joint-stock companies. Acts of Parliament were required for every line: there were five a year from 1827 to 1836, when the number jumped to twenty-nine. In the same year, parliament, trying to stop the growing 'railway mania,' limited loans to one-third of the chartered railways' capital, and it also banned any borrowing until half their share capital had been paid up. In the 1844 Railway Act, the state reserved the right to buy back any line that had operated for twenty-one years – a right that came in surprisingly useful during the nationalization mania a century later. It still did not stop the rush: there were 120 Railway Acts in 1845, 272 in 1846, and 170 in 1847 (involving some £40 million worth of capital).[18]

Although these companies were publicly traded, most of the real money for railways came from government and local businessmen (who had the most to gain from connecting their town to the network). 'We will venture to assert,' decided an 1835 circular to London bankers, 'that taking into account all the railways north of Manchester not one twentieth part of the capital was provided by members of the stock exchange.'[19] But the importance of tradable equities increased, particularly once the railways started issuing preference shares, which provided a guaranteed dividend rate (making their value easier to work out for investors), yet counted as equity under the government's debt-to-equity rules: by 1849, they accounted for two-thirds of the railways' share capital.[20]

Most of these shares were traded on local exchanges, such as Lancaster – out of reach of Lombard Street, which was still more interested in public debt than private equity. Railway mania was fanned by a growing number of railway papers, such as the *Railway Express*, *Railway Globe*, and *Railway Standard*. In its first issue in 1843, the *Economist* devoted less than a tenth of its 'commercial markets' column to money-market and stock prices. It bitterly condemned the railway speculation, forecasting a 'universal domestic affliction.' But in 1845 it launched its own highly profitable nine-page section, the *Railway Monitor*, professing that no financial paper could be without one.[21]

The railway was not the only force for change. By 1850, Britain had two thousand miles of telegraph lines. In 1845, Isambard Kingdom Brunel's *Great Britain* became the first propeller-driven boat to cross the Atlantic. As the British economy opened up, owner-managers felt less in control. 'Competition, competition – new invention, new invention – alteration, alteration – the world's gone past me. I hardly know where I am myself; much less where my customers are,' Uncle Solomon muses to Walter Gay in *Dombey and Son* (where the evil Carker, incidentally, is killed by a train). *Middlemarch* – set in a market town soon to be connected to the railway – was written by George Eliot in the 1870s, but it captures perfectly the sense of panic and possibility that modern technology engendered in the period.

THE GREAT VICTORIAN DEBATE

In the 1840s, politicians finally made real headway with Britain's confused company laws. Early in the decade, legal obfuscation helped produce an outbreak of fraudulent scams, involving not just railways but also the assurance companies that Dickens pilloried in *Martin Chuzzlewit* (1843). In 1844, William Gladstone, the president of the Board of Trade (and the sponsor of the restrictive Railway Act of the same year), pushed through the Joint Stock Companies Act. The 1844 act allowed companies to dispense with the need to get a special charter, and be incorporated by the simple act of registration.[22] But it did not include the crucial ingredient of automatic limited liability.

Limited liability was still anathema to many liberals. Adam Smith, remember, had been adamant that the owner-managed firm was a purer economic unit: the only way the joint-stock firm could compete was through the 'subsidy' of limited liability. Some of the industrialists who had helped get rid of the Corn Laws were suspicious.[23] Surely entrepreneurs could raise the necessary sums by tapping family savings and plowing back the firm's earnings? Wouldn't limited liability just impose the risk of doing business on suppliers, custom-ers, and lenders (a complaint that modern economists later echoed)? And wouldn't it attract the lowest sort of people into business? The majority of established manufacturers, most of whom were located far from London, were against the new measure.[24] So, according to Walter Bagehot, were the rich, who thought the poor would reap the biggest rewards.

There were voices on the other side, too. Denying business-people a commercial tool like limited liability was itself illiberal, argued some reformers. 'If people are willing to contract on terms of relieving the party embarking his capital from loss beyond a certain amount, there is nothing in natural justice to prevent it,' argued Robert Lowe to the Royal Commission on Mercantile Law.[25] John Stuart Mill and Richard Cobden argued that limited liability would help the poor to set up businesses. Mill continued to worry whether professional managers could ever match the zeal of owner-managers, but he decided that for large businesses, the only alternative to the joint-stock system was government control. Christian Socialists also rallied to limited-liability firms, seeing them as a way of both enriching the poor and reducing class conflict.

The government also was concerned about the less abstract question of losing business to foreign countries. In the early 1850s, some twenty English firms were established in France as *commandites par actions*, even though it cost as much as £4,000 to do this. 'So great is the demand for limited liability,' pleaded Edward Pleydell-Bouverie, the vice-president of the Board of Trade in 1855, 'that companies are frequently consti-tuted in Paris and the United States.'[26] Using these argu-ments, Pleydell-Bouverie forced through a Limited Liability Act in 1855, which granted the privilege of limited liability to incorpo-rated companies, as defined by the 1844 act, subject to various fiddly capital requirements. How the bill sneaked through par-liament is not entirely clear; one theory is that the Palmerston government wanted to claim that it had done something other than vote yet more money for the Crimean War.

Pleydell-Bouverie was then replaced by Robert Lowe, who masterminded the landmark Joint Stock Companies Act of 1856 (which removed the qualifications of the Limited Liability Act). If anyone deserves the title 'father of the modern company,' it is Lowe. Lowe was a complicated figure: a serious intellectual who made his career in the rough-and-tumble of politics and a fervent liberal who turned against giving the lower classes the vote during a visit to Australia.[27] He once caustically condemned a supporter of universal suffrage as being the sort of person 'whose idea of a joint-stock company is one in which everybody is a director.'[28] He famously promoted educational reform on the grounds that if Britain must have democracy, 'we must educate our masters.' It is a measure of his stature that Gladstone later made him Chancellor of the Exchequer, even though Lowe had ruined his cherished 1867 Reform Act.

Lowe, however, had no doubts about the merits of free

markets or of setting companies free from state control. 'To 1825 the law prohibited the formation of joint-stock companies,' he declared. 'From then to now it was a privilege. We hope to make it a right.' By then, he had rallied much of the liberal press to his cause. In an article entitled 'Why Companies Are Now Necessary' (July 19, 1856), the *Economist* admitted that 'it is very probable that companies will be carried to excess . . . but the state ought no more to interfere to stop the waste of capital, than to stop its judicious employment.' What the paper called 'the principle of Liberty' was all important.

Lowe's 1856 act allowed businesses to obtain limited liability with 'a freedom amounting almost to license.'[29] Banks and insurers were excluded; but there were no minimums for share capital. All that was needed was for seven people to sign a Memorandum of Association, for the company to register its office, and for the company to advertise its status by calling itself 'ltd.' It was this act, slightly modified, that was swept up into the comprehensive 1862 Companies Act that Gilbert and Sullivan celebrated in *Utopia Limited*.

This new regime was still a long way from modern shareholder capitalism. British law provided remarkably little protection for shareholders (who, for instance, did not need to be given audited accounts till 1900).[30] It was not until the case of *Salomon* v. *Salomon & Co. Ltd.* in 1897, when the House of Lords ruled in favor of an unsavory leather merchant who had transferred his assets into a limited company, that the separate legal identity of the company, and the 'corporate veil' of protection that it offered to its directors, was firmly established in the law. And many companies used partly paid shares – shareholders, for instance, paid in only 10 shillings for each £1 share; that meant that if the firm got into difficulties, the other 10 shillings would be called for. As late as the 1930s, some cotton mills listed on the London Stock Exchange had negative share prices, reflecting this unpaid liability.[31] Yet companies now started to appear – and fail – by the thousands. Between the acts of 1856 and 1862, almost twenty-five thousand limited-liability companies were incorporated. In the three years following the 1862 act, new issues averaged £120 million a year. More than 30 percent of the public companies formed between 1856 and 1883 obliged their critics by going bankrupt, many of them in the first five years of their existence.

The most spectacular was Overend, Gurney, a once revered finance house that fell on hard times in the late 1850s. The partners tried to solve their financial problems by floating the firm as a limited-liability company, but they were unable to avoid bankruptcy. The company's collapse on Black Friday in May 1866 led to a run on the banks and the collapse of a swath of other companies. The Bank of England had to raise interest rates to a crippling 10 percent for three months to deal with the financial mayhem – and some critics tried to reopen the debate about the company. 'With its luring but deceptive flag, 'limited,' it has been a snare and a delusion,' argued one old opponent, 'like the candle to the moth, or gunpowder in the hands of children.'[32]

Still, Europe's children were desperate to get hold of the new gunpowder. In May 1863, France, keen for its entrepreneurs to compete on equal terms, passed a law allowing businesspeople to establish joint-stock companies with full limited liability, provided that the capital involved did not exceed 20 million francs. Four years later, the limit was removed and general permission to form *sociétés anonymes* was granted. In 1870, Germany also made it much easier to found joint-stock companies. The result was a boom in company creation: 203 were set up in 1871, 478 in 1872, and 162 in 1873.[33]

A NEW SORT OF ORGANIZATION

Two points emerge clearly from all this activity. First, no matter how much modern businessmen may presume to the contrary, the company was a political creation. The company was the product of a political battle, not just the automatic result of technological innovation.[34] And the debate forged in mid-nineteenth-century Britain has shadowed the institution ever since: Is the company essentially a private association, subject to the laws of the state but with no greater obligation than making money, or a public one which is supposed to act in the public interest?

Businessmen might see the joint-stock company as a convenient form; from many politicians' viewpoint, it existed because it had been given a license to do so, and granted the privilege of limited liability. In the Anglo-Saxon world, the state might decide that it wanted relatively little in return: 'these little republics,' as Robert Lowe called them, were to be left alone. But other governments would demand more.

Second, the little republics plainly had a political and social impact in the societies that spawned them. As Peter Drucker puts it, 'This new 'corporation,' this new Société Anonyme, this new Aktiengesellschaft, could not be explained away as a reform, which is how the new army, the new university, the new hospital presented themselves. It clearly was an innovation. . . . It was the first autonomous institution in hundreds of years, the first to create a power center that was within society yet independent of the central government of the national state.'[35] The industrial economy's need for establishing economies of scale and scope would drive the big company to the forefront of capitalism and society – but it would do so most notably in the United States.

4 The Rise of Big Business in America
1862–1913

In the 1880s, Richard Sears was the station agent for the Minneapolis and St. Louis railroad in a small Minnesota town. Short of things to do, he began to peddle wood and coal to local farmers. When a local jeweler refused to buy a consignment of watches sent by a Chicago company, the enterprising young Sears stepped in, bought them, and sold them to other agents up and down the line. In 1887, he took the year-old R. W. Sears Watch Company to Chicago, linked up with an Indiana watchmaker, Alvah Roebuck, and went into the mail-order business, specializing in watches and jewelry. Like its Chicago rival, Montgomery Ward, the Sears, Roebuck catalogue offered rural America a way around expensive local retailers. By 1895 the Sears catalogue was 532 pages long, offering everything from guns to stoves.

Sears was a copywriter of genius, but the company would never have grown so big without the organizational talents of Julius Rosenwald, who became his partner in 1901 (Roebuck had sold out in 1894 for $25,000). One of the new breed of professional managers, Rosenwald tightened up the administration of the firm, censoring some of the founder's less truthful sales pitches and establishing a 'laboratory' for testing the products to check that they worked.

In 1906, the pair took the company public in order to raise more money. In the same year, the company opened a $5 million mail-order plant in Chicago, the largest business building in the world. To deal with the growing problem of fulfilling orders, Rosenwald developed a mechanical scheduling system, a sort of assembly line for customer orders. 'Miles of railroad tracks run lengthwise through and around this building for the receiving, moving and forwarding of merchandise,' boasted the Sears catalogue. 'Elevators, mechanical conveyors, endless chains, moving sidewalks, gravity chutes, apparatus and conveyors, pneumatic tubes and every known mechanical appliance for reducing labor, for the working out of economy and dispatch is to be utilized here in our great Works.'[1] One of the first people to visit this industrial marvel was reputedly Henry Ford. In 1916, Rosenwald added another innovation – a pension fund for employees in which the firm's contributions were tied to its profits and much of the fund was invested in Sears's stock.

The remarkable growth of Richard Sears's business from a hobby to a recognizably modern corporation, complete with shareholders, distinct operating units, a national network of suppliers, and professional salaried managers (not to mention management processes that would be 'benchmarked' by other industries), gives some idea of the revolution that took place in America in the late nineteenth century. It was not just a question of making use of the railroads. A firm structured like Sears, Roebuck in 1916, with thousands of employees, pensioners, and shareholders, did not exist in 1840 – not even in the wild imaginings of some futuristic visionary.

Back then, the bulk of economic activity was conducted through single-unit businesses, run and owned by independent traders, who would have been more familiar with the Merchant of Prato's business methods than Henry Ford's. When John Jacob Astor died in 1848, he was the country's richest man, leaving an estate valued at about $20 million. But even at the height of his business career, when he was running the American Fur Company, he never employed more than a handful of people, the most important of whom was his son. His 'headquarters' consisted of a few clerks working in a room the size of a hotel suite.

In 1840, businesspeople expected the work of coordinating their own activities with those of other businesspeople over a region as vast as the United States to be done by the market. Nobody would have thought that a single vast organization could coordinate, say, the demand for women's undergarments in Oregon with the production of cotton in New England.[2] Of course, most people throughout this period continued to work in small private businesses (such as farms). And there were also some industries, such as health care, which remained oddly resistant to economies of scale. But by the First World War, the giant corporation had become the dominant business institution in America: the gold standard by which all other enterprises were judged. It had also helped propel America to the top of the economic league. In 1851, at Queen Victoria's Great Exhibition, America failed to fill its allotted space, and the young monarch was unimpressed by 'their very curious inventions.'[3] By 1913, America produced 36 percent of the world's industrial output compared with Germany's 16 percent and Britain's 14 percent.[4]

The behemoths that were created in this period helped found modern America. It was their jobs that lured people from all over the world to America's big cities; their abuses that hastened the development of labor unions and antitrust law; their indifference to the environment that meant that sunlight could hardly penetrate the smoky air of Pittsburgh and Chicago; and their capacity to produce wealth that posed questions about inequality and meritocracy. The robber barons excited awe and disgust in equal measure for their 'conspicuous consumption' (a term that Thorstein Veblen first coined to describe their spending habits), in the form of mansions, parties, and art collections. Even the parsimonious Andrew Carnegie, whose writings included *The Advantage of Poverty*, owned a Scottish castle, Skibo, with a staff of eighty-two and a New York mansion with sixty-four rooms.[5]

FIRST CAME THE RAILROADS

Why did these extraordinary organizations take off when they did? Alfred Chandler has provided the classic answer: 'Modern business enterprise' became viable 'only when the visible hand of management proved to be more efficient than the invisible hand of market forces.' For that to happen, a new system of transport and communication was necessary.

The railroads were not just great enablers for modern business; they were also the first modern businesses.[6] It took gigantic quantities of capital – much of it from Britain – to build 31,000 miles of railroad, as America had in 1860 (let alone the 240,000 miles it had by 1910).[7] Railroads had equally little choice about being the first firms to employ large armies of full-time managers. Moving huge amounts of freight around the country without trains crashing into each other required an awful lot of administration. Initially borrowing from the British example (where the railways were typically run by retired army officers), the bigger railroads began to build up elaborate hierarchies, employing fifty to sixty managers by as early as 1850, and hundreds more thereafter.

These managers were new figures in an agrarian society: people who didn't own the organizations they worked for but nevertheless devoted their entire careers to them. They had a high sense of their calling (some even looked down on the mere amateurs who had founded the companies). And they pioneered many of the tools of the modern corporation. Railroad executives such as Daniel McCallum (in the 1850s) and Albert Fink (in the 1860s) devised the accounting and information systems needed to control the movement of trains and traffic, to account for the funds they handled, and to determine profit and loss for the various operating units.

Meanwhile, the railways' voracious requirement for capital did more than anything else to create the modern New York Stock Exchange. In the 1830s, a good day on the Exchange might have seen a few hundred shares changing hands (on March 6, 1830, the worst day in its history, only thirty-one shares were traded). By the 1850s, with the railways booming, that figure ballooned to hundreds of thousands.[8] In 1886, it had its first million-share day.

From the end of the Civil War to the 1890s, Wall Street existed almost exclusively to finance the railroads, something investors often regretted. Rogues like Daniel Drew made their name manipulating the stocks of railroads like the Erie. (One song went, 'When Uncle Dan'l says Up/Erie goes up/When Uncle Dan'l says Down/Erie goes down/When Uncle Dan'l says "Wiggle waggle"/Erie bobs both ways.')[9] When another speculator, Jay Cooke, failed to sell bonds in the Northern Pacific Railroad, his bank collapsed on 'Black Thursday,' September 18, 1873, prompting scores of other bankruptcies and shutting the Exchange for ten days. In the last quarter of the nineteenth century, more than seven hundred railroad companies, which together controlled over half the country's rail track, went bankrupt.[10]

Yet, as in Britain, it was the railways that spawned an investor culture. The *Commercial and Financial Chronicle*, founded in 1865, and later the *Wall Street Journal*, founded in 1889, covered railroad stocks in depth. Henry Varnum Poor (Alfred Chandler's grandfather) edited the *American Railroad Journal* and then *Poor's Manual of Railroad Securities* before giving his name to the ratings agency Standard & Poor's.

Railroads accounted for 60 percent of publicly issued stock in America in 1898, and the proportion was still above 40 percent in 1914. But most of the money the railroads raised was debt, partly because the founders wanted to retain control and partly because bonds were more easily marketed abroad than equity. In 1913, there was $11.2 billion worth of railroad bonds, versus $7.2 billion of common stock, and that ignores both the railroads' enormous bank debts and the fact that half of the common stock was corporate cross-holdings.[11] Preference shares were also enormously popular – particularly after they were used to launch the Pennsylvania Railroad in 1871.

Such a narrow equity base made bankruptcy a common threat, spurring consolidation. Many of the earliest railway lines did not yet connect to each other. Bullies like Cornelius Vanderbilt and then J. P. Morgan tidied up this fragmented system. Even without their prompting, many railroad tycoons decided that collusion was the only way to ensure a regular flow of traffic and avert ruinous price wars.

This consolidation meant that by the 1890s, the railways were bigger than the utility companies that brought light, heat, and water to Chicago and New York, and bigger by far than the armies that defended the United States. In 1891, the army, navy, and marines employed a total of 39,492 people. The Pennsylvania Railroad employed over 110,000. The country's total gross national debt was $997 million – only $155 million more than the Pennsylvania's capitalization of $842 million.[12]

This concentration of power caused a backlash. But these

giants also helped build much of the infrastructure of a modern economy. The railroads provided the right-of-way for telegraph and telephone lines. They revolutionized the Post Office. They ended up owning most of the country's steamship lines. Above all, the railways brought a far-flung country together, making it possible to move large quantities of goods around the country both quickly and predictably. By the 1870s, the three weeks it took to move goods from Philadelphia to Chicago had been cut to a couple of days. And for some commodities, such as grain, it was not just a case of creating national markets but (thanks to similar improvements in shipping) creating global ones. By 1914, the Americas were exporting 600 million bushels of wheat to Europe, fifteen times the figure for 1850.

THE RETAILERS BEFORE THE MANUFACTURERS

The first American companies to take advantage of the railway infrastructure were in distribution and retailing.[13] In 1840, most goods were distributed around the country through a system of wheeling and dealing. Within a generation, distribution was dominated by giant companies. The 1850s and 1860s saw the appearance of huge wholesalers who bought directly from producers and sold to retailers. Then the 1870s and 1880s saw the birth of modern mass retailers – of chain stores, department stores, and mail-order companies.

The new retailers, typified by Julius Rosenwald, mastered the trick of reducing costs while improving choice. They turned over their stock at a far greater speed than their smaller rivals (always the secret of success in retailing). They set up huge purchasing departments and introduced new technology rapidly (witness the Sears mail-order plant). The pioneering department stores remained household names in their respective cities for the next century or more: Macy's, Lord & Taylor, and B. Altman in New York; Marshall Field and Carson, Pirie, Scott in Chicago; Emporium in San Francisco. Soon they were joined by retailers who were building national brands. Frank Woolworth opened seven small department stores in southeast Pennsylvania in the early 1880s. By 1909, he had more than three hundred stores in the United States and was opening branches in Britain.

Manufacturing was slower to catch on. The Civil War gave America's factories their first big spurt: the number of manufacturing companies jumped by 80 percent in the 1860s. Thereafter, the main spur for change was new technology – particularly electricity and later the internal combustion engine. But new technology was not much good without organizational change. For instance, the pioneers of using electricity in factories simply replaced steam with electricity without reorganizing the production process; it was only when factories started using electricity to power individual machines that productivity soared – something that did not happen in many cases until the mid-1920s.[14]

One of the first industrialists to reengineer production was Andrew Carnegie (1835–1919). Carnegie, a Scottish immigrant who came to embody the ideal of the self-made man, learned about management working for the Pennsylvania Railroad, and his first company, the Keystone Bridge Works, sold rails and bridges to the railways. In his factories, Carnegie introduced the 'line production' system, arranging his machines and workers into a sequence that allowed jobs to be broken down into their component parts. Where possible he tried to standardize things, and he ruthlessly exploited the advantages of scale. The more steel he could produce, the lower his costs; the lower his costs, the more he could sell. 'To make ten tons of steel would cost many times as much as to make one hundred tons,' he argued.

'The larger the scale of the operation, the cheaper the product.'[15] By 1900, a dozen men on the floor of a mill could roll three thousand tons of steel a day, as much as a Pittsburgh mill in 1850 rolled in a year. Car-negie's employees were organized in layer upon layer of managers, from foremen to direct his gangs of workers, to mill and furnace managers, to money managers, salesmen, marketing specialists, and two dozen partners with equity in his firm.

The line production system was perfected by Henry Ford (1863–1947). Ford's engineers borrowed particularly from the 'stopwatch' ideas of the first great management guru, Frederick Taylor, whose *Principles of Scientific Management* was published in 1911. They designed improved machinery, such as conveyors, rollways, and gravity slides, to assure the regular flow of materials. Their stroke of genius was to introduce conveyor belts to move parts past the workers on the assembly line. This reduced the time it took to make a Model T from twelve hours to two and a half hours. By the spring of 1914, Ford's Highland Park plant had reduced the time to one and a half hours, and it was turning out a thousand cars a day.[16] The frenetic world that was parodied in Charlie Chaplin's *Modern Times* had arrived.

ALL UNDER ONE ROOF

Ford's success was not just about building cars more swiftly, but also about bringing both mass production and mass distribution under the roof of a single organization. An 'integrated' industrial firm could find economies of scale in everything from purchasing to advertising – and thus pump an endless supply of cigarettes, matches, breakfast cereals, film, cameras, canned milk, and soup around the country. The key was to own as much of the process as possible. Ford even owned the land on which grazed the sheep that produced the wool that went into his seat covers.

Integrated companies, which did not really exist in the 1860s, dominated America's most vital industries by the turn of the century.[17] Typically, like Ford, they combined technological innovation with market clout. In 1881, James Buchanan Duke, who had a tobacco business in Durham, North Carolina, decided to get into the cigarette business – at the time regarded as something of a dead end. But Duke found a secret weapon – the Bonsack cigarette machine, which could turn out 125,000 cigarettes a day, at a time when the fastest worker could produce no more than 3,000. Duke's machines were soon producing far more cigarettes than the then-undeveloped market could absorb, so he created a huge marketing organization to pump up demand. Duke himself invented a crush-proof packet to make the smoker's life (or what remained of it) more convenient. He built his own purchasing, curing, and storing facilities to ensure a regular supply of raw materials. In 1890, he merged with four competitors to form the giant American Tobacco Company.

Duke's story was repeated in several other industries. George Eastman invented not only a cheap camera but also the idea of the amateur photographer to find a market for his photographic film. But the most distinctive feature of all the integrated firms was a desire to grow as big as possible. That inevitably led to mergers.

Cornelius Vanderbilt had already shown the benefits of consolidation in the railway industry. Between 1890 and 1904, huge waves of consolidation left most of the country's industrial base in the hands of around fifty organizations – usually (if sometimes unfairly) referred to as trusts. The merger era produced

THE RISE OF BIG BUSINESS IN AMERICA

some of the most powerful companies of their time, includ-ing U.S. Steel, American Cotton, National Biscuit, American Tobacco, General Electric, International Harvester, AT&T, and United Fruit. Two people are synonymous with the trust era: John D. Rockefeller (1839–1937) and J. P. Morgan (1837–1913).

Right from the beginning, Rockefeller realized the impor-tance of scale. In his first few years as an Ohio refiner, he bought fifty refineries in Cleveland and eighty in Pittsburgh, adding warehouses and timber yards (to make his own barrels) and ships (to transport them). In 1870, hoping to take advantage of a recession to expand further, he formed a joint-stock company, Standard Oil, distributing shares mainly among his original partners, and admitting a handful of new investors. He also set up the South Improvement Company, a cartel of refiners and railroads in Pennsylvania and Ohio, which squeezed out his competitors, effectively leaving him in charge of all Cleveland's refineries.

The South Improvement Company, which was chartered in Pennsylvania, was one of the first trust companies. Trusts, which separate the holding and control of assets from their ben-eficial ownership, were an old legal concept dating back to the Crusades (when knights left their possessions in the 'trust' of others, to be administered on their behalf in their absence). For the robber barons, they were a way of getting around primitive antitrust laws prohibiting companies from owning shares in each other. Shareholders in a number of competing companies gave their voting shares to a central trust company in return for tradable trust certificates bearing the right to receive income but not to vote. This gave the central body the ability to deter-mine common prices for the entire group.

In 1882, the Standard Oil alliance, a loose federation of forty companies, each with its own legal and administrative identity (to satisfy individual state laws), metamorphosed into the Standard Oil Trust. The new trust acquired a single headquarters – at 26 Broadway in New York City – and immediately set about rationalizing the oil industry. The company's costs fell dramatically, from 1.5 cents for refining a gallon of oil to 0.5 cents. 'The Standard was an angel of mercy,' Rockefeller argued, 'reaching down from the sky, and saying, "Get into the ark. Put in your old junk. We'll take all the risks!" '[18] Soon a quarter of the world's production of kerosene came from just three giant refineries.

Things then took an odd turn. One evening in 1889, Ohio's attorney general, David Watson, found a book in a Colum-bus bookstore called *Trusts: The Recent Combinations in Trade*, which included Standard Oil's trust deed as an appendix. Watson realized that Standard Oil of Ohio had been violat-ing its state charter by handing over control to out-of-state trustees. Ignoring a series of heavy-handed threats and, it is said, fulsome bribes, he sued, and in 1892, the Ohio Supreme Court ruled in his favor, renouncing the trust agreement and saying that the trust had created a monopoly.

Standard's bold response – that the only effect 'will be to inconvenience us a little' – was partly true.[19] Rockefeller now had an excuse to begin moving his empire to New Jersey, which in 1889 had created the most liberal incorporation law in the country, with politicians even setting up a company to handle the paperwork. The New Jersey law allowed for holding compa-nies – umbrella companies that own a controlling proportion of the voting shares of subsidiary companies. In 1899, after a number of legal feints, Standard Oil of New Jersey became the oil giant's formal holding company, controlling stock in nine-teen large and twenty-one smaller companies.[20] Big companies have used this device ever since (indeed, lawyers will doubtless point out that many of the huge companies that we mention henceforth are technically no more than legal shells).

Standard was only one of many trusts and big businesses to move to New Jersey. By 1901, two-thirds of all American firms with $10 million or more of capital were incorporated in the state, allowing New Jersey to run a budget surplus of almost $3 million by 1905 and paying for a rash of new public works. Inevitably, other states fought back. Virginia turned itself into what one legal treatise called a 'snug harbour for roaming and piratical corporations.' The New York legislature was forced to enact a special charter for the General Electric Company to prevent it from absconding to New Jersey. But the big winner of this particular 'race to the bottom' would be Delaware. By the time the Great Depression struck, the state had become home to more than a third of the industrial corporations on the New York Stock Exchange: twelve thousand companies claimed legal residence in a single office in downtown Wilmington.[21]

Most of the other industrial trusts converted to holding companies, too. They, unlike Rockefeller, often did so at the instigation of the most powerful trust of them all, the 'money trust,' as Congressman Charles Lindbergh dubbed the masters of Wall Street. Since the United States had no central bank, J. P. Morgan and a few other bankers wielded enormous power. The bankers made use of the new holding companies themselves to get around rules preventing them from investing in shares (Morgan, for instance, controlled a Philadelphia broker, Drexel and Company). Whereas most of the earlier industrial mergers were the work of company founders (Vanderbilt in railways, Charles Pillsbury in flour), the turn-of-the-century merger boom was, if anything, the work of 'stock promoters.'

This marked a turning point, because it tied industrial companies to the stock market. In 1890, fewer than ten manufacturing shares were traded on the main exchanges – and most of those, like Pullman's Palace Car Company, were closely associated with railroads. Investors regarded industrial firms as risky. Industrialists hung on to the equity in their companies themselves, raising money through family connections and commercial loans rather than the capital markets.

Morgan engineered an extraordinary change. The total amount of capital in publicly traded manufacturing companies increased from $33 million in 1890 to more than $7 billion in 1903. The new giants included industrial combines such as General Electric and International Harvester, but most emblematic was the metamorphosis of the world's largest manufacturer, Carnegie Steel, into the still more gargantuan U.S. Steel.

Carnegie had founded his company with his own money, amassed speculating on the railroads. Claiming a profound distrust of public ownership ('Where stock is held by a great number, what is anybody's business is nobody's business'), he structured his corporation into a series of partnerships, each controlled by Carnegie himself, and subject to an overall 'Iron Clad Agreement' that forced any partner who wanted to get out to sell his stake back to the company at book value.[22] But in 1901, after a brief conversation on a golf course, he sold the company to J. P. Morgan and Elbert Gary for $480 million. They then combined it with another two hundred or so smaller firms and offered the United States Steel Corporation to the public at a valuation of $1.4 billion. A similar deal done today, expressed as the same proportion of GNP, would approach half a trillion dollars. [23] U.S. Steel accounted for two-thirds of America's steel production and employed a quarter of a million men. The company's value was equivalent to two-thirds of all the money then in circulation in the United States.[24]

The U.S. Steel issue was another turning point in the development of the American company. Henceforth, the privately held industrial firm would be the exception – the main one being the Ford Motor Company. That did not mean that a recognizably modern equity market emerged immediately. Equity trading remained a clubbish affair until at least the end of the First World War.[25] Most investors still found it diffi-cult to value shares, often focusing on dividend yields: even relatively sophisticated people talked about buying 5 per-cent shares till the Second World War. Auditing was also lax: in 1914, an attempt to force all industrial companies to produce uniform accounts was defeated in Congress.

THE BACKLASH

Were these new companies making America a better place? The robber barons themselves found heartwarming justification for their doings in the Social Darwinism of Herbert Spencer, an English thinker who won a huge following in America for his doctrine of 'the survival of the fittest' and his opposition to state intervention of all sorts, from tariffs to public education. 'Light came in as a flood, and all was clear' was Carnegie's reaction to Spencer. Rockefeller likened laissez-faire capitalism to breeding an American Beauty rose 'by sacrificing the early buds which grew up around it. This is not an evil tendency in business. It is merely the working out of a law of nature and a law of God.'[26]

Others saw this pruning from the other side. In 1869, the historian Charles Francis Adams wondered whether the joint-stock corporation wasn't a dangerous idea. Society had 'created a class of artificial beings who bid fair soon to be masters of their creator. It is but a few years since the existence of a corporation controlling a few millions of dollars was regarded as a subject of grave apprehension, and now this country already contains single organizations which wield a power represented by thousands of millions . . . they are already establishing despotisms which no spasmodic popular effort will be able to shake off.'[27]

In fact, a considerable popular effort was amassing. As the new companies changed society, so society changed the companies. One example was the growth of labor unions. The earliest American unions were fairly small affairs, most of them based on particular crafts and concentrated among skilled workers. But the consolidation of capital prompted a consolidation of labor. The National Labor Union appeared in 1866. Another organization, the Knights of Labor, boasted 700,000 workers at its peak in 1886. The 1890s marked a maturing of the unions as well as a maturing of big business – and a series of bloody confrontations between the two.

The bloodiest standoff came at Andrew Carnegie's steel plant in the quaintly named Homestead, Pennsylvania. Car-negie claimed to be a friend of workingmen, even encouraging his employees to call him 'Andy.' But in 1892, he and his plant manager, Henry Clay Frick, engineered a confrontation with the Amalgamated Association of Iron, Steel and Tin Workers, then the strongest union in the American Federation of Labor, with 24,000 members across the country. In the past, the union had served Carnegie's purpose by imposing equal labor costs on his competitors. Now that those competitors had been beaten, it was an inconvenience. Carnegie cut the men's wages – a decision that precipitated a strike and then a lockout. Frick duly built a three-mile-long stockade around the factory, complete with barbed wire, searchlights, and two hundred shooting holes for rifles. He also employed three hundred men from the Pinkerton detective agency to protect his strikebreakers. The workers won the first round, with the Pinkertons surrendering after a pitched battle, which claimed sixteen lives. But they lost the war. The governor sent in eight thousand state militia. Frick brought in strikebreakers, many of them blacks who were banned from joining the union, and smashed the strike.

The Homestead strike, and the bloody Pullman strike of 1894, where the attorney general (a railroad shareholder, as it happened) intervened to declare that the American Railroad Union was 'an illegal combination' under antitrust laws, showed the gulf between the power of capital and labor. In all kinds of disputes, the courts tended to uphold the notion of freedom of contract rather than workers' rights. Yet, between 1897 and 1904 union membership multiplied almost fivefold. In 1906, the AFL began to focus on electoral politics, supporting Democratic Party candidates and forming close relations with the big political machines that now dominated city politics. Union bosses seized on tragedies like the Triangle Shirtwaist Company fire in New York in 1911 to agitate for safer working conditions. In 1914, the Wilson administration granted unions immunity from antitrust suits, and in 1916, it passed a series of bills that restricted working hours and child labor.

Politicians also slowly succumbed to popular pressure to break up the empires of the 'malefactors of great wealth.' The 1890 Sherman Antitrust Act broke new ground by defining monopolies but failed to set out many ways of punishing or preventing them (and was used against the unions). Public opinion demanded more. In 1902, Ida Tarbell, the first great muckraking journalist, began a nineteen-part exposure of Standard Oil in *McClure's* magazine, arguing that the company's rise had been accomplished by 'fraud, deceit, special privilege, gross illegality, bribery, coercion, corruption, intimidation, espionage or outright terror.' Meanwhile, up in Boston, 'the people's attorney,'

Louis Brandeis, skewered Morgan over his stewardship of the New Haven Railroad.

In 1906, Teddy Roosevelt's administration launched a successful antitrust suit against Standard Oil, and in 1911, the Supreme Court ordered it to be broken up, creating indirectly the forerunners of Exxon, Amoco, Mobil, and Chevron. The next year, Morgan was summoned to the hearings into the money trust convened by Congressman Arsène Pujo. The Pujo committee concluded that the money trust held 341 directorships in 112 companies with assets of $22 billion.[28] In 1913, after Morgan died, his directors quietly resigned at forty of the companies. America also set up a central bank in 1913, making the money trust less powerful. In 1914, the Clayton Antitrust Act restricted interlocking directorships, but only when they restrained trade.

THE POPULARITY OF THE COMPANY

Yet, the backlash against the corporation was far less powerful than many people had hoped. By European standards, America was hesitant about reining in the corporation. The courts did strike down the most egregious examples of monopoly: for instance, American Tobacco, which by 1911 controlled 150 factories with a capitalization of $502 million, was split up that year into several separate companies. But most of the other huge combines – the Nationals, the Generals, and the Americans – discovered that, with a little diplomacy, they could hang on to most of their fiefdoms.

Most Americans were ambivalent about business. They disliked concentrations of corporate power – the United States, after all, is based on the division of power – but they admired the sheer might of business. They disliked the wealth of businessmen, but they admired the fact that so many of them came from nothing – that Rockefeller was the son of a snake-oil salesman and Carnegie began his career as a telegraph messenger. In 1867, E. L. Godkin produced an explanation of why America lacked the intense class consciousness of Europe that probably remains true to this day: 'The social line between the laborer and the capitalist here is very faintly drawn. Most successful employers of labor have begun by being laborers themselves; most laborers . . . hope to become employers.' Strikes, he added, were a matter of business, not sentiment.

Three things kept ambivalence about the corporation from tipping into hostility. The first was that the big companies wised up to politics. When politicians first began to regulate business, William Vanderbilt, Cornelius's son who had inherited his empire in 1877, famously retorted that 'the public could be damned.' But the company became a much more active participant in politics. The Senate became known as the 'millionaires' club,' more representative of different economic interests than the individual states: there were lumber senators, silver senators, etc. Mark Hanna (1837–1904), a Cleveland steel magnate, became Republican National Chairman and helped to make William McKinley president. And companies began to hire public-relations advisers, notably Ivy Lee (1877–1934), who almost managed to smooth over the Rockefellers' brutal suppression of the 1913–1914 miners' strike against the Colorado Fuel and Iron Company.[29]

But it was not all just spin. The second thing was the growth of what would now be called corporate social responsibility. As we have already seen, Rosenwald thought it was good business to set up a pension fund for Sears workers. Many other big companies made positive efforts to cement the bond between capital and labor. U.S. Steel, for instance, spent $10 million a year on employee welfare programs – 'to disarm the prejudice against trusts,' as the chairman of the board informed his colleagues. International Harvester established a profit-sharing plan.[30] Company towns sprang up across America. Some were brutal prison camps; many more were prompted by what Henry Mills, a Unitarian minister in Lowell, called 'the sagacity of self-interest.' Well-housed and well-educated workers would be more efficient than their slum-dwelling, feckless contemporaries. For instance, in 1880, George Pullman built his eponymous town on the outskirts of Chicago in the hope that a 'rational and aesthetic order' would elevate the character of the workers. The town, which was later to become a battleground during the 1894 strike, was not to everybody's liking, not least because it was largely teetotal. But it was hailed by one American newspaper 'as handsome as any wealthy suburban town'; a British newspaper even dubbed it 'the most perfect city in the world.'

Meanwhile, the robber barons embraced philanthropy. By 1919, the Carnegie Endowment alone had spent over $350 million (more than $3 billion in current dollars) on a huge variety of projects, including 2,811 public libraries and 7,689 church organs. No doubt many philanthropists were inspired by a genuine desire to do good or to atone for past sins, but social ambition also played its part in putting businessmen on the path of civic virtue – as a glance at the history of Philadelphia demonstrates.

The City of Brotherly Love was one of the most snobbish in the country. Yet, the city's old families were not foolish enough to turn their backs on the new wealth that was being created by the Pennsylvania Railroad and the nearby coalfields.[31] Instead, an informal deal was struck with the corporate parvenus: they could enter 'society' so long as they were willing to shoulder their social obligations. This transformation of red-blooded capitalists into proper Philadelphians involved buying a house in Rittenhouse Square, playing golf at the Merion Cricket Club, perhaps even fox-hunting at the Whitemarsh Valley Hunt Club, and certainly handing their daughters (and their dowries) to the sons of the more gentrified families. Above all, it involved civic involvement – organizing charities, serving on the boards of the symphony, the art museum, and the University of Pennsylvania. Charles Curtis Harrison, one of the city's great businessmen, became president of the University of Pennsylvania.[32] Wharton Business School was set up by Joseph Wharton, founder of the Bethlehem Iron Company.

This concentration of power was hardly democratic. Philadelphia's elite thought nothing of deciding the fate of the city in their oak-paneled clubs. Yet, by co-opting big business into the city's future, the old elite plainly brought much good to their city. And it was repeated across the entire country. The wealth that the new companies of the 1880s and 1890s generated was not just wasted competing to get invited to Mrs. Astor's parties or forcing robber barons into the *Social Register* (first issued in 1888), though both these things certainly happened. It also helped to establish social services where none existed. It built museums and art galleries in a country that was prone to philistinism. And it bound the classes together in a society where the income gap was widening.

The third and most important thing that provided a bedrock of support for the company came down to a simple proposition: The company was making America richer. In his essay 'Why Is There No Socialism in the United States?,' Werner Sombart, a German sociologist, argued that 'on the reefs of roast beef and apple pie socialist utopias of every sort are sent to their doom.' The new companies plainly improved the living standards of millions of ordinary people, putting the luxuries of the rich within the reach of the man in the street. When Henry Ford went into the car business, it was devoted to handcrafting toys for the super-rich; by 1917, he had sold 1.5 million Model T's. When George Eastman purchased his first camera in November 1877, it cost him $49.58, and was so difficult to use that he had to pay $5 for lessons. But, by 1900, the Brownie automatic cost $1 and was marketed under the slogan: 'You push the button and we do the rest.'[33]

The productivity of these companies was usually tied to gigantism, which also raised barriers to market entry. The only way to compete with one of the huge companies was to build a huge new company of your own. Even if you could raise the cash and recruit the right managers, you risked introducing so much new capacity onto the market that the whole market would crash. This, rather than anything to do with collusion, remained the underlying reason why a handful of huge companies dominated their respective industries from the 1880s to at least the 1940s.

*The Rise of Big Business in Britain,
Germany, and Japan*
1850–1950

The United States may have bounded ahead of the rest of the
world, but other countries were also trying to come to terms
with companies. The three most interesting, Britain, Germany,
and Japan, illustrated different approaches to the new economic
form. Britain, despite its wholehearted enthusiasm for laissez-
faire, was a reluctant convert to companies. Germany and Japan
embraced the idea much more warmly, but tried to twist it to
rather different ends, such as workers' welfare and the quest for
national greatness. Companies in Germany and Japan were
there to serve 'society,' while their Anglo-Saxon competitors
chased profits. The much-ballyhooed gulf between shareholder
capitalism and stakeholder capitalism had already opened up.

LAND OF HOPE AND HISTORY

With Britain, one question predominates: Why didn't it exploit
companies better? After all, Britain led the way in industrialization, and in the development of relatively large firms. In 1795,
Sir Robert Peel, the largest cotton manufacturer in the country,
owned twenty-three mills in the north, some of which
employed as many as five hundred people.[1] Britain was also a
pioneer in setting companies free from state control. Yet, in the
late nineteenth century, it failed to produce the big industrial
firms that were then the key to economic success.

In 1902, America's manufacturing workforce was only marginally bigger than Britain's, but Britain had few firms to rival America's leviathans. As we have seen, U.S. Steel was worth $1.4 billion, and the company employed a quarter of a million people. The largest British employer, Fine Cotton Spinners and Doublers, only had thirty thousand workers, and the largest firm on the stock market, Imperial Tobacco, was worth only £17.5 million. Britain's top hundred firms only accounted for about 15 percent of output in 1900.[2]

There are plenty of reasons for Britain's failure to capitalize on its head start. As a pioneer of industrialization, it was tempted to cling to earlier forms of capitalism; as a compact island, it was under less pressure to produce corporate giants (though the empire constituted a 'domestic' market as big as America). Two things stand out: the country's strong preference for family firms and personal management; and the British prejudice against industrial capitalism.

British entrepreneurs clung to the personal approach to management long after their American cousins had embraced professionalism. As late as the Second World War, a remarkable number of British firms were managed by members of the founding families. These founders kept the big decisions firmly within the company, only calling on the help of professional managers *in extremis*. Family-run firms had no need for the detailed organization charts and manuals that had become commonplace in large American companies. They relied instead on personal relations and family traditions.

This was not necessarily a ticket to the boneyard. The Cadbury family maintained their hold over their chocolate firm while making all the appropriate investments in production, sales, and advertising – indeed, it was better run than its American peer, Hershey Foods. As late as the Second World War, the owners of Cadbury managed and the managers owned. Others were not so wise. For instance, Pilkington, the glassmaking giant, reserved all its top positions for members of the family. But by the end of the 1920s, the assembled Pil-kingtons were no match for the sheer complexity of running a modern company. Profits were falling. Austin Pilkington, the chairman, was cracking under the strain, unable to craft a long-term strategy. The family took remedial action, bringing outsiders onto the board and dragging younger Pilkingtons off to management-training courses, but by that time, it had sacrificed much of its lead in the glass industry.[3] The firm was saved only because it had the good luck to recruit a talented man who rejoiced in the surname Pilkington but turned out to be no relation whatsoever.

As we shall see, the big British firms that did eventually emerge turned out to be longer-lasting and more profitable than their big American peers. The problem was there were not enough of them. The vast majority of family firms were far too small to thrive in a world dominated by the economies of scale and scope. Britain boasted more than two thousand cotton firms – John Maynard Keynes complained that 'there is probably no hall in Manchester large enough to hold all the directors' – but only a handful had anything as sophisticated as a marketing department. The steel industry was dominated by family firms that could barely keep their heads above the waters in their domestic market, let alone swim in foreign seas.

In a famous essay, Donald Coleman argued that the curse of corporate life in Britain was the distinction between 'gentlemen' and 'players.' Far too many talentless amateurs rose to high positions, and far too many talented professionals were kept in the ranks. This lack of managerial expertise cost them dearly. For instance, at the end of the First World War, British armsmakers such as Vickers regarded the diversification into peacetime products as a way to find work for their existing workers and factories, rather than as a chance to modernize the company. Unlike, say, Du Pont, Vickers failed to invest in research and development or to build up its marketing machine.

This reflected a difference in philosophy. For American industrialists, companies were almost an end in themselves. They were to be tended and grown. For British industrialists, they were a means to a higher end: a civilized existence. They were there to be harvested. Before the First World War, for example, the ratio of dividends to earnings in Britain was as high as 80 to 90 percent, far higher than in the United States.

This points to the second British problem with companies: a fatal snobbish distaste for business. The elite public schools steered their most talented students into conspicuously useless subjects like the classics and poured scorn on anything that smacked of commerce. ('He gets degrees in making jam/ at Liverpool and Birmingham' went one popular Edwardian rhyme.) The state schools and new universities all did their best to emulate the antiutilitarian bias of Eton and Oxbridge. George Orwell noted that the ideal products of this educational system 'owned no land, but . . . felt that they were landowners in the sight of God and kept up a semi-aristocratic outlook by going into the professional and fighting services rather than into trade.'[4]

To British intellectuals, particularly between the wars, a career in business was a despicable way of life, pursued only by the stupid and unimaginative. One of C. P. Snow's characters remarks that 'successful business was devastatingly uninteresting.'[5] 'How I hate that man' was C. S. Lewis's tart comment on Lord Nuffield, Oxford's biggest employer and one of the most generous benefactors to Lewis's beloved university.[6] J. B. Priestley dismissed 'the shoddy, greedy, profit grabbing, joint-stock company industrial system.'[7] Almost everyone blamed industry for polluting the countryside, debasing the culture, and shattering their peace and quiet.

This antiutilitarian bias robbed British companies of both scientific expertise and managerial brainpower. The proportion of students studying science at British universities ac-tually *declined* between the wars – from 19 percent in 1922 to 16 percent in 1938. Those students who did risk social ostracism by studying science mimicked the antiutilitarian bias of their colleagues in the humanities. In opening a new set of laboratories at Bristol University in 1927, Lord Rutherford made it clear that he would regard it as an 'unmitigated disaster' if they were devoted to 'research bearing on industry.'[8] Only four of the seventy-one new science chairs created between 1925 and 1930 were in technology.[9]

Still, science was positively revered compared with business education. Britain produced no more than a handful of departments of business and accounting, and those that it did produce studiously avoided any contact with the business world. 'Practical courses in salesmanship are conspicuous by their absence,' noted Abraham Flexner, an American observer in 1930. 'The teaching staff are not unfamiliar with American developments, but they are out of sympathy with them. They do not pretend to be practical men capable of advising business concerns; no member of the business or commerce faculty at Manchester has any remunerative connection with industry . . . they have also found that successful businessmen have nothing to tell their students.'

The upshot of all this was that British companies were starved of both able recruits and up-to-date expertise. A survey of Cambridge graduates in 1937–1938 revealed that fewer sons followed their fathers into business than into any other calling:

only 23 percent of men from business families went into business themselves.[10] Industry had to make do with the runts of the litter – people who had failed to make it into university or the professions. Inevitably, they often justified their own poor training by disparaging 'foreign methods,' such as economics, industrial psychology, or accountancy. In the 1930s, no more than a dozen big British manufacturers had management training schemes for university graduates.

The horror of things industrial even manifested itself in the development of British company towns. Embarrassed by the filthy, crowded, and chaotic cities that gave birth to the Industrial Revolution, some of the best British companies embraced Ebenezer Howard's idea of the 'garden city' – a new decentralized social order, in which people would be rural enough to keep in touch with the land but urban enough to support such civic institutions as hospitals, concert halls, and art galleries. George Cadbury (1839–1922) moved his factory to Bourneville, on the fringes of Birmingham, to escape from the 'unwholesomeness of city life.' The town was generously supplied with parks; each worker had a large garden, which his lease required him to maintain. Joseph Rowntree (1836–1925), another Quaker chocolate king, built New Earswick, a traditional-looking village that, as one of its architects put it, 'gave life just that order, that crystalline structure it had in feudal times.' William Lever, the soap baron, was even keener on giving his model town, Port Sunlight, a preindustrial feel, getting his architects to construct replicas of well-known Tudor and Elizabethan buildings, including Anne Hathaway's cottage.

Still, no amount of anticorporate activity could keep Britain locked in the Middle Ages. Companies profoundly changed British life. They prompted the development of trade unions (who founded the Labour Party in 1900). They revolutionized working habits. They provided career opportunities for a whole class of people who had been denied it before – women. In the fifty years after 1861, the number of female clerical workers increased five-hundred-fold (compared with a fivefold increase for men). Mostyn Bird's 1911 novel, *Women at Work*, showed how city offices were transformed by these new clerical workers: 'In the morning, at nightfall and in the luncheon hour women pour in and out of every block of office buildings in numbers that rival men. The City is no longer the man's domain.'[11]

THE GOOD AND THE FEW

The picture was not all so dark. As we shall see in chapter 7, British firms, for all their idiosyncrasies, were still more internationally oriented than American businesses. And there was also an elite of advanced British companies that realized there was far more to be gained from mastering change than resisting it.

A continual prompt for this was the stock market, one area where the British preserved their lead over the Americans. As early as the 1880s, companies in shipping, iron, and steel began to use the London market to raise capital to finance new technology, such as steel ships. In 1886, Guinness was floated as a public company. Companies, spurred on by professional share promoters like Gilbert and Sullivan's Mr. Goldbury, made it easier for smaller investors to get into the market by issuing lower share denominations. In 1885, only about sixty domestic manufacturers and distributors were listed; by 1907, the figure was almost six hundred.

Interestingly, the few big firms that Britain managed to produce by 1912 proved (over the long term, at least) to be more successful than their American peers.[12] Imperial Tobacco, a loose federation of family firms, might have looked far less impressive than James Duke's huge American Tobacco, but by 1937, it had grown to four times the size: Imperial was more successful at converting smokers to branded cigarettes from other forms of tobacco, and better at promoting internal competition within the company.[13] Similarly, British Petroleum outperformed Exxon over the long term, and J&P Coats did better than American Woolen.

Some historians have speculated that the few big firms that Britain did produce by the First World War were hardened by free trade, in a way that American firms were not. Going public was also a stimulus to better performance, as J&P Coats showed. By the end of the First World War, a small sewing-thread firm, based in out-of-the-way Paisley, had become one of Britain's biggest manufacturers, thanks to the family's prescient decision in the 1880s to dilute their family ownership by floating their stock. The merger boom that followed the First World War led to a rapid increase in the number of quoted companies: there were 719 of them by 1924 and 1,712 by 1939. By the early 1920s, 57 percent of Britain's corporate profits came from public firms – a figure that would gradually rise to 71 percent by 1951.

Coats, Shell, and Imperial Tobacco were part of a small elite of modern companies, including Distillers, Courtaulds, Guest Keen & Nettlefold, and Guinness. The two most influential were both the products of mergers: Imperial Chemical Industries and Unilever. ICI, which brought together four British firms in 1926, had impressively multicultural roots. Its main component was Brunner Mond, which had been set up a half century earlier in Cheshire by a German from Cassel (Ludwig Mond) and a Swiss (J. T. Brunner); it also included the explosives business of Alfred Nobel.[14] The driving force behind the

1926 merger was Sir Alfred Mond (1868–1930). An early advo-
cate of health insurance and profit-sharing, Mond had even
earned the gentle mockery of T. S. Eliot ('I shall not want
Capital in Heaven/For I shall meet Sir Alfred Mond./We two
shall lie together, lapt/In a five per cent. Exchequer Bond'). ICI
adopted a version of Alfred Sloan's multidivisional structure
(see chapter 6), employed an army of professional managers,
developed close links with the country's universities, and began
to take the battle to Du Pont. By 1935, it had around fifty thousand workers, the same number as Guest Keen & Nettlefold, an
emerging metals and engineering giant.

Yet, Britain's biggest manufacturing employer, with sixty
thousand workers, was Unilever. Lever Brothers remained
firmly under the thumb of William Lever until his death in
1925. Lever's road to greatness allegedly began in the 1880s,
when he heard a customer ask whether the shop had any more
of his 'stinking soap': Sunlight soap built the firm, not to
mention Port Sunlight. Lever decimated his domestic rivals by
doing such ungentlemanly things as advertising his products.
But his business decisions became increasingly erratic after the
war (he bought the United Africa Company for several million
pounds without knowing what it did). After he died, a professional manager, Frances Darcy Cooper, took over, and at the end
of the decade, the firm merged with a Dutch rival, Margarine
Unie.

The newly created Unilever became a ruthlessly efficient
marketing machine, adapting products to tastes (the English
liked salted margarine; continental Europeans didn't) and
attacking Procter & Gamble in its home territory. In 1936, it
attacked Crisco, P&G's dominant vegetable oil, by giving away
free cans of its new brand, Spry, which it claimed was 'extra-
creamed'; this made for dubious science, but it sounded good

enough to force P&G to claim that Crisco was 'double-creamed,' prompting Lever to claim that Spry was triple-creamed. Even though Procter finally trumped that with super-creamed Crisco, Spry's sales reached half those of Crisco.[15]

This diversion into vegetable oils is meant to underline a simple point: when Unilever fought against Procter & Gamble or ICI took on Du Pont, it was as equals. Britain's tragedy was that ICI and Unilever were the exceptions rather than the rule. It was not until after the First World War that Britain belatedly developed big firms in the 'second industrial revolution' businesses (steel, chemicals, and machinery). However, such firms could indeed be built outside the United States – as Germany and Japan showed.

THE RISE OF GERMAN INDUSTRY

Germany was not unified until 1871. Yet, over the next forty years, its great companies enabled it to replace Britain as Europe's leading industrial power. In the late nineteenth century, the finest examples of the 'new economy' in Europe were all in Germany: the vast electrical-equipment producing complex at Siemenstadt, the huge chemical works of Leverkusen, Ludwigshafen, and Frankfurt, the massive machinery works and steel mills in the Ruhr and along the Rhine. When Alfred Krupp died in 1887, his company employed twenty thousand people, and boasted its own hospitals and schools. Britain had nothing comparable to offer.

Germany's companies were similar to America's in their focus on the new economy: almost two-thirds of the top two hundred dealt with metals, chemicals, and machinery. But they embodied a rather different sort of capitalism – one that emphasized cooperation rather than competition and that gave a leading role to the state. By 1900, four clear structural differences were apparent between the German corporate model and its Anglo-Saxon equivalent.

The most obvious was Germany's tolerance of what Anglo-Saxons would regard as anticompetitive practices. German law did not prohibit 'combinations in restraint of trade' like British law. Nor did it possess any antimonopoly legislation like America's Sherman Antitrust Act. In 1897, the year that the American Supreme Court ruled that the Sherman Antitrust Act was constitutional, its German equivalent ruled that contractual agreements regulating prices, output, and market share could be enforced in courts of law, because such agreements benefited the country as a whole. They were, in essence, a form of 'cooperative self-help.'

This nationalistic outlook was underpinned by the works of Friedrich List (1789–1846). List, a somewhat eccentric figure who might be caricatured as the Prussian answer to Adam Smith, spent much of his life in exile in the United States. In *The National System of Political Economy* (1841), he argued that the basic economic unit is not the individual but the nation: the job of businesspeople and politicians is to band together for the national good. His ideas were enthusiastically promoted first by Prussian politicians, and then by leaders of the newly unified Germany. For the Junker aristocracy that ran Imperial Germany, businesses were there to provide power for the great war machine; of course, they were supposed to work together.

The economic downturn of 1873–1893 helped force German companies together: the number of cartels rose from a mere four in 1875 to 385 in 1905.[16] Cartels ranged from informal 'gentlemen's agreements' to highly legalistic syndicates. The 'model cartel' was the Rhenish-Westphalian Coal Syndicate, which regulated production and prices and which operated, in various guises, from 1893 to 1945, once counting as many as ninety companies among its members. *Interessengemeinschaften* or 'communities of interest' were coalitions of firms that pooled profits and coordinated policies on everything from patents to technical standards. Members of such 'IGs' were also frequently tied together by cross-shareholding.

I. G. Farben is a good example. It began as a loose alliance of young chemical firms (including Bayer and Hoescht) that cooperated through cartels, then evolved first into a 'community of interest' and finally, in 1925, into a properly integrated company. By the late 1930s, I. G. Farben controlled 98 percent of Germany's dyestuffs, 60 to 70 percent of its photographic film, and 50 percent of its pharmaceuticals. Yet, company policy was still dictated by a series of committees that looked suspiciously like the boards of its individual constituents. I. G. Farben also had a whole series of cross-shareholdings, joint ventures, and pricing agreements with other German chemical firms.

The second difference from Anglo-Saxon capitalism was the influence of the big banks. Germany's capital markets were too localized and inefficient to power its industrialization. Germany's bankers stepped into the breach by forming joint-stock and limited-partnership banks that duly channeled money from savers of all sorts, first into the railways (which were financed by bank debt, not bonds) and then, after the railways were nationalized in 1879, into young industrial companies like Siemens. The biggest were the 'universal banks' that managed to be commercial banks, investment banks, and investment trusts all rolled into one. (J. P. Morgan achieved something similar, but only by getting around state laws, rather than being encouraged by them.) Deutsche Bank (formed in 1870) and Dresdner Bank (1872) concentrated on financing large-scale industry, leaving smaller banks to concentrate on the *Mittelstand* of medium-sized family firms that also powered the country's success.

In 1913, seventeen of the biggest twenty-five joint-stock companies were banks. Universal banks financed almost half of the country's net investment. Bankers also sat on the supervisory boards of all Germany's great industrial companies, providing advice and contacts as well as capital (it was the bankers that organized Siemens's merger with German Edison in 1883). Their power was magnified by proxy voting rights, which allowed them to vote the shares of all their other investors, an arrangement that made hostile takeovers almost impossible to execute.[17]

The bankers' influence was reflected in the third big difference vis-à-vis the Anglo-Saxon world: Germany's two-level system of corporate control. The 1870 law that introduced free incorporation also obliged joint-stock companies to have two levels of control: management boards, responsible for day-to-day decisions, and supervisory boards, made up of big shareholders and assorted interest groups – not just banks but also local politicians, cartel partners, and, eventually, trade unions. The supervisory board gained even more power in 1884.

All these structural differences – the boards, the bankers, and the legalized collusion – reinforced the fourth distinguishing thing about German companies: the emphasis on their social role. German stakeholder capitalism, as we suppose it must be called, was partly influenced by the German guilds, which had survived much longer than their counterparts in other parts of Europe and had preserved the vital system for apprenticeships (which helps explain the German fascination with training). At first, social responsibility was voluntary. Alfred Krupp introduced pensions and health and life insurance for his workers as early as the 1850s. But from 1883 to 1889 Bismarck imposed a comprehensive 'social insurance' system on companies, forcing them to pay pensions; in 1891, he introduced a system of 'code-termination,' giving a formal voice to workers on companies.

The result was that German companies were much keener on cooperating with trade unions than their Anglo-Saxon rivals. Individual employers might clash with trade unions, sometimes bitterly so. But there was nevertheless a powerful belief that, in an ideal world, all interests ought to be involved in decision-making. Factory foremen were regularly consulted by managers (a trend that translated into military success in the First World War: the German army gave far more power to non-commissioned officers). In 1920, laws were passed setting up works councils giving workers an even louder voice. The Third Reich (1933–1945) abolished trade union powers. But even under Hitler, Germans clung to their belief in consulting society's various interest groups, albeit in a perverted form. The Nazi-sponsored German Labor Front helped to improve working conditions in factories and even initiated cheap holiday excursions.[18]

The interesting question with Germany is how much this markedly different idea of the company helps to explain its undoubted economic success. The huge upheavals of the first half of the twentieth century only increase the suspicion that Germany got something big right: its companies had to endure, among other things, defeat in two world wars, several chronic recessions, Nazism, and partition. Our suspicion is that Germany's success owed less to stakeholder capitalism than to two rather more practical things.

The first was the cult of education – particularly scientific and vocational education. This was there from the very first.[19] Peter Drucker claims that the foundation for Germany's manufacturing productivity was laid in the 1840s by August Borsig (1804–1854), an early industrialist who pioneered corporate apprenticeships, mixing on-the-job experience and formal class-work.[20] Universities – particularly technical universities – happily acted as both research agencies and recruiting grounds for local industries.[21] By 1872, the University of Munich alone had more graduate research chemists than the whole of England. The Berlin Institute offered a two-year course in how to establish and manage factories.[22] Germany began to found business schools at about the same time as the United States, in 1900. Boring-sounding industry groups such as the Association of German Engineers (1856) actually provided consulting advice and disseminated technical knowledge. German firms also pioneered the development of internal laboratories, and invested heavily in research and development even in such basic industries as coal, iron, and steel.[23]

The second related area was the respect accorded to managers, who enjoyed the same high status as public-sector bureaucrats. (Lower-level managers were even called 'private civil servants.') In Britain, where even the most senior salaried executives were often referred to as 'company servants,' only a few managers were admitted to boards of directors by 1920. In Germany, salaried managers dominated supervisory boards.[24] German companies also made a point of giving technicians managerial responsibility rather than just relying on generalists, as Americans tended to.[25]

THE *ZAIBATSU* OF JAPAN

Japan's version of organized capitalism had many similarities to Germany's. Japan also leaped ahead in the 1870s – and Japan also embraced a conception of the company that combined up-to-date professionalism with a pronounced and sometimes atavistic nationalism.

In 1868, the shogunate that had ruled the country for more than 250 years collapsed, and power reverted to the sixteen-year-old emperor Meiji – or rather to the officials and oligarchs who surrounded him. Some of the *samurai* who supported the restoration hoped that the emperor would cleanse the country of barbarians. Instead, the ruling oligarchs decided to open the country to the West as part of their 'rich country, strong army' policy. They invited more than 2,400 foreigners from twenty-three different countries to provide instruction in Western methods. Employment of foreign experts accounted for about 2 percent of government expenditure.[26]

The state forced the *samurai* to shed their feudal ways and wear Western clothes. It also created business opportunities by selling state-owned factories for a song, introducing joint-stock-company laws, abolishing the guilds and other restrictions on occupational choice, and preaching that moneymaking was perfectly compatible with Shinto and Buddhist religious beliefs, as well as being downright patriotic. Many *samurai* reinvented themselves as businessmen, often starting companies with the compensation money they were given for giving up their military duties.

The young companies had the advantage of being able to learn from their predecessors' mistakes. The growth was explosive. In 1886, nearly two-thirds of the yarn in Japan was imported; by 1902, it was virtually all home-produced; by the First World War, Japan accounted for a quarter of the world's cotton-yarn exports. Japanese firms were particularly good at electrification. By 1920, half the power in Japanese factories came from electric motors, compared with less than a third in America and barely a quarter in Britain.

The government undoubtedly played a leading role in Japan's great leap forward. The Ministry of Industry regarded its role as making up for 'Japan's deficiencies by swiftly seizing upon the strengths of the western industrial arts.' It did so in all sorts of ways – by pouring money into infrastructure, establishing universities, directing business and credit toward companies, and establishing public companies as recipients of Western technology and models of Western business. Government investment usually exceeded private-sector investment until the First World War. It was a government official who introduced a venture capitalist to a university teacher who had the wild dream of building a power station. The result was the Tokyo Electric Light Company, the ancestor of Toshiba. Shibusawa Eiichi, who founded the Dai Ichi bank, which financed many of the original joint-stock companies, worked for a spell in the Ministry of Finance. Mitsui liked to compare itself to the British East India Company. Mitsubishi, Mitsui's great rival, owed a great deal to government subsidies for shipping. In 1894, the firm repaid the favor by lending its ships to the military to wage war with China.

Mitsubishi was the model for the *zaibatsu* – the Japanese conglomerates (literally, 'financial cliques') that dominated business in the country until the Second World War (and were subsequently reborn as *keiretsu*). These conglomerates were a strange mixture of feudal dynasties, old-fashioned trading companies, government agencies, and modern corporations. At the heart of each *zaibatsu* sat a family-owned holding company that controlled a cluster of other firms through cross-shareholdings and interlocking directorates. Each cluster typically included at least one bank and insurance company as a conduit for public savings. Managers were typically recruited into the holding company from university. Thereafter, they spent the whole of their lives within this extended family of companies.

The companies that made up each *zaibatsu* operated in a bewildering number of industries, but their lack of focus did not prevent them from being highly competitive. At its best, the *zaibatsu* structure allowed for great flexibility: businesses could specialize in particular markets, but also summon up economies of scale when they needed them. The groups were also kept in shape by the rivalry between them. By the end of the Second World War, the four biggest ones – Mitsui, Mitsubishi, Sumitomo, and Yasuda – controlled a quarter of the paid-in capital of Japanese firms.[27] As in Germany, small firms still existed – according to the 1930 census, 30 percent of Japan's manufacturing output came from factories with fewer than five workers – but the tone was set by the *zaibatsu*.

The *zaibatsu* were particularly successful in mixing family ownership with meritocratic management. The founding families were understandably nervous about the joint-stock concept, initially trying to keep control through special classes of shares, and then after those were banned in the 1890s, making arrangements so that groups of descendants could hold shares together (and banning them from selling them). Control of Mitsubishi alternated between two branches of the Iwasaki family. The founder's brother insisted that 'although this enterprise calls itself a company and has a company structure, in reality it is entirely a family enterprise.'[28] At Mitsui, ownership was split among five branches of the same family.

Yet, the same families were notably better than, say, the British at handing over day-to-day management to professionals. The tradition of hiring a professional manager (*banto*) to run the family business dated back to the eighteenth century. Leading Japanese industrial families also proved remarkably adept at transforming feudal loyalty into corporate loyalty:

samurai who were willing to die for their masters became loyal company men who were willing to do anything for company success (and who were given lifetime employment in return). By the early 1930s, almost all the *zaibatsu* had handed over control of their management to well-trained professionals. A 1924 survey of the 181 largest Japanese companies found that 64 percent of top executives held a college degree or equivalent, a higher proportion than in the United States at the time.[29]

In both Germany and Japan, the government's habit of steering the economy in pursuit of national greatness reached an ugly zenith in the Second World War. One history nicely describes the Nazi approach to business, where small companies were pushed into a limited number of huge industrial groups in the service of the national business machine, as 'Listian economics gone berserk.'[30] The *zaibatsu* looked like feudal relics to Douglas MacArthur, who broke them up after the war. MacArthur had no doubt where to find the best model for the corporation: it was in the United States of Coca-Cola and General Motors.

6 *The Triumph of Managerial Capitalism*
1913–1975

By the outbreak of the First World War, the big company had become a defining institution in American society: the motor of one of the most rapid periods of economic growth in history; a dominating figure in political life; and a decisive actor in transforming America from a society of 'island communities' into a homogenous national community. Thanks largely to its embrace of this extraordinary institution, the American century was under way.

Different forms of company continued to sprout around the world. We have discussed Britain's family firms and Japan's *zaibatsu*; a longer book could have dwelled on the charms of France's huge utility companies or northern Italy's networks of small businesses. Even in America, the economy was upset by the discontinuities of war, recession, and the New Deal, not to mention continuous technological changes that provided opportunities for smaller companies to leap forward and for old giants to trip up. Who remembers Central Leather, the Nevada Consolidated Group, or Cudahy Packing?[1]

All the same, the most remarkable thing about the sixty years after the First World War was continuity – particularly the continued success of big American business. A list of America's biggest companies in 1970 would have seemed fairly familiar to J. P. Morgan, who died in 1913. Yet, this very predictability, this sameness, was itself the result of one important innovation, introduced in the 1920s: the multidivisional firm.

The multidivisional firm was an important innovation by itself, because it professionalized the big company and set its dominant structure. But it was also important because it became the template for 'managerialism.' If the archetypical figure of the Gilded Age was the robber baron, his successor was the professional manager – a more tedious character, perhaps, but one who turned out to be surprisingly controversial. In the 1940s, left-wing writers like the lapsed-Trotskyite James Burnham argued that a new managerial ruling class had stealthily obliterated the difference between capitalism and socialism; in the 1980s, corporate raiders said much the same thing.

SLOAN'S REVOLUTION

In the first two decades of the twentieth century, a silent takeover began: the gradual separation of ownership from control. The robber barons may have kept the big strategic decisions in their own hands, but they couldn't personally oversee every detail of their gigantic business empires. And they couldn't find the management skills that they needed among their immediate families, who anyway found more amusing things to do: Digby Baltzell writes acidly about 'the divorcing John Jacob Astor III (three wives), Cornelius Vanderbilt, Jr. (five wives), Tommy Manville (nine wives) or the Topping brothers (ten wives between them).'[2] So the company founders turned to a new class of professional managers.

The likes of King Gillette, William Wrigley, H. J. Heinz, and John D. Rockefeller hired hordes of black-coated managers to bring order to their chaotic empires. America's great cities were redesigned to provide these managers with a home – the new vertical filing cabinets known as skyscrapers. In 1908, the Singer Company built the world's tallest building in New York to house some of these managers (it was 612 feet high), only to be outbuilt eighteen months later by Metropolitan Life (700 feet), which was then trumped in its turn by the Woolworth Building (792 feet).

The inhabitants of these towers began by doing the boring work of coordinating the flow of materials from suppliers to eventual customers. But soon their organizational skills – Singer's mastery of door-to-door selling – became decisive competitive advantages in themselves. And, gradually, these 'Company Men' began to make the big strategic decisions as well. Every merger required the central management staff to rationalize the acquired business. Every robber baron's death freed their hands. Every share issue dispersed ownership: the number of ordinary shareholders rose from 2 million in 1920 to 10 million in 1930.

This was the background to the multidivisional firm that Alfred Sloan (1875–1966) pioneered at General Motors. Like many other young companies, GM was caught out by the recession of 1920. The company's founder, William Durant (1861–1947), whom Sloan later described as 'a great man with a great weakness – he could create, but not administer,' controlled almost all of the company's activities, supported by a rudimentary staff. GM was saved by Pierre du Pont (1870–1954), who bought 37 percent of the struggling carmaker. He in turn picked Sloan, a young engineer who was then managing GM's parts and accessories units, to redesign the organization from top to bottom.

Sloan, who became GM's president in 1923, was the prototypical organization man, the first manager to be famous for just that. 'Management has been my specialization,' he wrote flatly in his autobiography.[3] Du Pont and Sloan decided that the company's activities were too disparate to be run by a single central authority. Instead, they decided to treat its various units – its car, truck, parts, and accessory businesses – as autonomous divisions. Each division was defined by the market that it served, which in the case of cars was determined by a 'price pyramid': Cadillac for the rich, Oldsmobile for the comfortable but discreet, Buick for the striving, Pontiac for the poor but proud, and Chevrolet for the plebs. By providing a car 'for every purse and purpose,' the pyramid allowed GM to retain customers for their whole lives.[4] It also ameliorated the economic cycle. In boom times, like the late 1920s, GM could boost profits with high-end products; in busts, like the 1930s, it could rely on Chevys.

Yet, if Sloanism was built on decentralization, it was controlled decentralization. The divisions were marshaled together to use their joint-buying clout to secure cheaper prices for everything from steel to stationery. And Sloan and Du Pont created a powerful general office, packed full of numbers men, to oversee this elaborate structure, making sure, for example, that the divisions treated franchised salesmen correctly. Divisional managers looked after market share; the general executives monitored their performance, allocating more resources to the highest achievers. At the top, a ten-man executive committee, headed by Du Pont and Sloan, set a centralized corporate strategy.

The beauty of Sloanism was that the structure of a company could be expanded easily: if research came up with a new product, a new division could be set up. 'I do not regard size as a barrier,' Sloan wrote. 'To me it is only a problem of management.' Above all, the multidivisional firm was designed, in Sloan's words, 'as an objective organization, as distinguished from the type that get lost in the subjectivity of personalities.' In other words, it was not Henry Ford.

Ford's determination to administer his huge empire himself pushed it toward disaster. He ignored both the new science of market segmentation and the wider discipline of management theory. (He let it be known that anyone found with an organization chart, however sketchily drawn, would be sacked on the spot.)[5] He deliberately engineered a destructive conflict between his son and one of his most powerful lieutenants, drove many of his most talented managers out of the company, and refused to put even the most elementary management controls in place. One department calculated its costs by weighing a pile of invoices; the firm was hit with a $50 million tax surcharge for excess profits during the Second World War because no one had filed the necessary forms for war contractors.[6] By 1929, Ford's share of the market had fallen to 31 percent while General Motors's had risen from 17 percent to 32.3 percent.[7]

There was an irony in the inventor of the assembly line being himself outorganized. As one historian, Thomas McCraw, puts it, 'What Ford did for physical machines, Sloan did for human beings.'[8] The multidivisional structure, which was progressively adopted by many of America's marquee names, including General Electric, United States Rubber, Standard Oil, and U.S. Steel, was an ideal tool for managing growth. The Du Pont Company, for instance, initially diversified haphazardly into a succession of promising new products, including paints, dyes, film, and chemicals. But it overloaded its centralized management system – so much so that the only bit to make money was its old explosives business. Once it copied GM's example, and began to create separate divisions to manage its various businesses, the new entities began to make money too. By 1939, explosives accounted for less than 10 percent of its income.

Du Pont also illustrated another advantage of Sloan's system: it institutionalized innovation by making it the responsibility of specific people. Du Pont poured money into research, supporting not just specialized laboratories in its various divisions but also a central laboratory, known as 'Purity Hall,' which concentrated on fundamental research. By 1947, 58 percent of Du Pont's sales came from products that had been introduced during the previous twenty years.[9]

Even companies that were less directly influenced by Sloan embraced his creed of professional management. In 1927, Coca-Cola's researchers began a three-year study of fifteen thousand places where the drink was sold in order to work out things like the exact ratio between sales volume and the flow of people past their product. Similar scientific studies, under the research-obsessed Robert Woodruff (1889–1985), led not just to bottled Coke being sold in garages, but to strict rules about the color of trucks (red) and the sort of girls to put in ads (a brunette if there was only one girl in the picture). Sales duly soared.

Over at Procter & Gamble, the company also plowed a fortune into ever more professional marketing, inadvertently ruining modern culture by creating the soap opera (as the radio dramas sponsored by the firm came to be called). On May 13, 1931, an uppity P&G recruit named Neil McElroy broke the in-house prohibition on memos of more than one page, producing a three-page suggestion for the company to appoint a specific team to manage each particular brand. 'Brand management' provided a way for consumer-goods firms to mimic Sloan's multidivisional structure.[10]

Such discipline became even more essential during the 1930s. By July 1932, the Dow Index, which had stood at 386.10 on September 3, 1929, had fallen to 40.56. Industrial output fell by a third. In the Depression, consumers were only willing to part with their surplus cash for genuine novelties (or apparent ones: by the late 1930s, Procter alone was spending $15 million a year on advertising). Yet, throughout this turmoil, the big Sloanist firms held on to their positions. With the barriers to entry in most businesses still high, they were rarely threatened by young upstarts; the main danger was of a neighboring giant diversifying systematically into their territory. The only way a multidivisional firm could get beaten was by another multidivisional firm.

THE MANAGERS

Behind this success sat a new culture of management. In the late nineteenth century, business education consisted of little more than teaching bookkeeping and secretarial skills. Only the University of Pennsylvania's Wharton School, founded in 1881, offered stronger stuff. But business schools began to spread. Harvard Business School opened its doors in 1908, the same year that the Model T started rolling off the assembly line. By 1914, Harvard was offering courses in marketing, corporate finance, and even business policy.

Management thinkers also began to follow the trail blazed by Frederick Taylor (1856–1915). Arthur D. Little was the first of a new class of management consultants, soon followed by James McKinsey, who set up shop in 1926, three years after the American Management Association was founded. Even politicians joined the craze: Herbert Hoover tried to apply scientific management to government.

From the very first, these management thinkers offered contradictory advice. A rival 'humanist' school, including Mary Parker Follett (1868–1933) and Elton Mayo (1880–1949), challenged Taylor's dominant 'rationalist school,' arguing that the key to long-term success lay in treating workers well. In 1927, a group of behavioral scientists, including Mayo, began an epic ten-year study of Western Electric's Hawthorne Works in Chicago (which among other things proved that turning lights on and off improved productivity).

Yet, even these softer thinkers were still apostles of the new management religion. 'Management not bankers nor stockholders is the fundamental element in industry,' claimed Follett. 'It is good management that draws credit, that draws workers, that draws customers. Whatever changes should come, whether industry is owned by capitalists, or by the state, or by the workers, it will always have to be managed. Management is the permanent function of business.'

Follett's claim might be taken as a tribal manifesto for one of the unsung heroes of the twentieth century. Company Man has not had a good press. Sinclair Lewis pilloried him as *Babbitt* (1922), the epitome of self-satisfied philistinism. In *Coming Up for Air* (1939), George Orwell portrayed him as little more than a wage slave – 'never free except when he's fast asleep and dreaming that he's got the boss down the bottom of a well and is bunging lumps of coal at him.' Yet he helped to change companies the world over.

As early as 1920, Company Man's character had been formed by two things: professional standards and corporate loyalty. Company Man was defined by his credentials rather than by his lineage (like the upper classes) or his collective muscle (like the workers). He was part of a professional caste that adopted Frederick Taylor's motto that there was 'the one best way' for organizing work and sneered at rough-hewn entrepreneurs for not knowing it.

But this class solidarity was balanced by loyalty to his employer. The first rule at Standard Oil, according to one contemporary, was that every employee must 'wear the 'Standard Oil' collar. This collar is riveted on to each one as he is taken into 'the band,' and can only be removed with the head of the wearer.'[11]

Thomas Watson, the salesman who created the modern IBM in 1924, built his organization out of Company Men.[12] He located the firm in a small town, Endicott, in New York State, the better to lay down the law. IBM men wore a uniform of dark suit and white shirt, refrained from strong drink, sang the praises of the founder in a company song, and competed for membership in the 100 percent club, an elite club open to only the most successful salesmen. They could even listen to an IBM symphony commissioned by the founder. On IBM Day, in 1940, some ten thousand IBM-ers converged on the New York World's Fair in special trains. Watson argued that such loyalty 'saves the daily wear and tear of making daily decisions as to what is best to do.'

This paternalism went much lower than the officer class. Modern debates about shareholder capitalism often obscure the fact that many of the best Anglo-Saxon companies have happily shouldered social obligations without much prompting from government. Procter & Gamble pioneered disability and retirement pensions (in 1915), the eight-hour day (in 1918) and, most important of all, guaranteed work for at least forty-eight weeks a year (in the 1920s). During the Depression, the company kept layoffs to the minimum and the company's boss, Red Deupee, cut his own salary in half and stopped his annual bonus. Henry Ford, who fumed that when he hired a pair of hands he got a human being as well, became a cult figure around the world by paying his workers $5 a day – well above the market rate. Henry Heinz paid for education in citizenship for his employees.

THREE DEBATES THAT DEFINED THE COMPANY

As the company's role in society deepened, so did the debate about that role. Three works published in the 1930s and 1940s asked fundamental questions about this awkward institution: Why did companies exist? Whom were they run for? And what about the workers?

The most basic of these three works began as a lecture in 1932 to a group of Dundee students by a twenty-one-year-old economist just back from a tour of American industry. Five years later, Ronald Coase published his ideas in a paper in *Economica* called 'The Nature of the Firm.' Coase tried to explain why the economy had moved beyond individuals selling goods and services to each other. The answer, he argued, had to do with the imperfections of the market and particularly to do with transaction costs – the costs sole traders might incur in getting the best deal and coordinating processes such as manufacturing and marketing.

The history of the company since 1850 validated Coase's point. General Motors, for instance, reaped enormous economies of scale by bundling together plenty of transactions that had previously been done independently. The costs of, say, trying to negotiate each bit of steel that was needed for a car would have been prohibitive. Yet, GM still dealt with independent franchisees. Coase nicely quotes an earlier British economist, Dennis Robertson (1890–1963), who talked about the relationship between 'conscious' firms to the 'unconscious' market as being like 'lumps of butter coagulating in a pail of buttermilk.' GM might have been a huge chunk of butter, but it was still within a liquid churn.

The second book, *The Modern Corporation and Private Property*, by Adolf Berle and Gardiner Means, published in

1932, outlined the distribution of corporate wealth in America. Like the Pujo committee that had harried Morgan twenty years earlier, Berle and Means found plenty of evidence of great concentration: the top two hundred companies accounted for half the total assets; AT&T alone controlled more assets than the twenty poorest states. But the new oligopolies were owned not by robber barons but by 10 million ordinary shareholders. Carnegie's gibe about 'anybody's business becoming nobody's business' had come true.

Companies were supposed to be run in their owners' interest. In 1916, the Michigan Supreme Court had famously ruled (in a case that two minority shareholders, the Dodge Brothers, had brought against Henry Ford) that 'a business corporation is organized and carried on primarily for the profit of the stockholders.' Berle and Means argued that the passivity of these millions of shareholders had frozen 'absolute power in the corporate managements.' In economic terms, the interest of the agent was separate from that of the principal. Of course, managers had often been uppity people, inclined to know best. (Asked to slow down by the onboard merchants, one Dutch East India Company captain, Jacob van Heemskerck, barked back, 'When we risk our lives, the Lords of the Company may damn well risk their ships.')[13] And, of course, theorists had always considered the separation of ownership from control. But Berle and Means were the first to identify corporate governance as a practical problem.

Henceforth, rather than worrying about monopolistic entrepreneurs squeezing out smaller businesses, the authorities increasingly looked for ways to protect small investors from the power of unfettered managers. In 1933, the New York Stock Exchange finally required proper accounts for listed companies. The Securities Acts of 1933 and 1934 placed the fiduciary responsibility for reporting accurate information firmly with directors. Roosevelt created the Securities and Exchange Commission in part as a weapon against the bankers who he thought bore much of the blame for the recession. (He also established a flotilla of regulatory agencies to police companies, bringing trucking firms, airlines, and utilities under federal direction.)

The last book was about General Motors itself. In 1942, Sloan's attention was caught by Peter Drucker's *The Future of Industrial Man* (1942), which argued that companies had a social dimension as well as an economic purpose. Sloan invited the Viennese exile, still at the time regarded as something of a misfit who didn't know whether he was a political theorist or an economist, to analyze GM. The result was *The Concept of the Corporation*, published in 1946.

The book, one of the best managerial tomes ever written, roams freely, worrying, for instance, about both the percentage of Victorian Englishmen who were gentlemen (a minute fraction, in Drucker's view) and the efficiency of Russian industrial management. The book had plenty of positive things to say about Sloan. Drucker argued that big was beautiful, and that GM's decentralized structure was the key to its success.[14] Indeed, his commendation persuaded countless firms to follow suit.

But there was a sting in the tail. *The Concept of the Corporation* made a passionate plea for GM to treat workers as a resource rather than just as a cost. In 'the assembly-line mentality,' warned Drucker, workers were valued purely in terms of how closely they resembled machines.[15] In fact, the most valuable thing about workers was not their hands, but their brains. The importance of empowering workers became more important when Drucker identified a new class of 'knowledge workers' (as he dubbed them in 1959). These were lessons that

Japanese managers (who read Drucker's work assiduously) learned rather more quickly than GM. The carmaker's attempt at talking to its workers came down to suggesting they write an essay, 'My Job and Why I Like It.'

CORPORATE IMPERIALISM

One sign of the success of managerial capitalism is the way that it co-opted its state equivalent after 1945. During the Second World War, governments tightened their grip on business. In Germany, Krupp and I. G. Farben became adjuncts of the Nazi war machine. In America, the federal government bought as much as half of the products of both industry and agriculture. Wartime governments everywhere ordered management and labor to collaborate in order to boost productivity and prevent the strikes that had marred the 1930s.

This relationship continued after the war, though under different guises on each side of the Atlantic. In America, big government remained an important ally of big business, frequently drafting businesspeople (United States secretaries of defense included Neil McElroy, the P&G memo writer who later became the firm's boss; Charles Wilson, Sloan's successor at GM; and Bob McNamara from Ford). The Cold War saw the creation of what Dwight Eisenhower dubbed 'the military industrial complex.' Some of the biggest companies in the country – such as 'the Generals' – relied heavily on the Pentagon. Even smaller companies sent lobbyists to Washington to drum up contracts and shape regulation. Nevertheless, the government remained a customer, a policeman, and an ally, not an owner.

That was not the case in Western Europe, where postwar governments systematically nationalized companies that controlled the 'commanding heights' of the economy: heavy industry, communications, infrastructure. In many countries, one in five workers were employed by nationalized companies. Their founders liked to claim that they were creating a new form of socialist company. Herbert Morrison, the architect of Britain's postwar nationalization, argued that 'the public corporation must be more than a capitalist business, the be-all and end-all of which is profits and dividends. Its board and its officers must regard themselves as the high custodians of the public interest.'

Yet, the prophets of nationalization shared the Sloanist belief in managerialism and gigantism. Politicians like Morrison claimed that they could manage things better than the anarchic market, with stricter controls and forward planning. Family firms were too small to survive in a world dominated by the economies of scale and scope. Nationalized companies would be big enough to capture economies of scale, to mobilize resources, and adopt new technology. They would be run by trained professionals rather than bumbling amateurs. Instead of just making their new fiefdoms into government departments, most nationalizers stuck to the corporate model. 'These are going to be public corporations, business concerns,' explained Morrison; 'they will buy the necessary brains and technical skills and give them their heads.'

European and Asian governments poured resources into 'national champions' – companies that were either owned by the state or closely aligned to it. Italy's national oil company, ENI, for example, rapidly developed into a sprawling conglomerate that included some thirty-six businesses, dabbling in everything from crude oil to hotels. Even when they were not steering contracts toward these corporate pets, politicians found other ways to protect them. Heavy government regulation and intervention made it hard for newcomers to break into the status quo. Many countries saw the creation of a revolving door between big companies and big government. France's *énarques*, the elite bureaucrats from the École Nationale d'Administration, glided between the 'private' and public sectors with well-oiled ease.

Seen in this light, state-owned companies were less threats to Sloanism than heavy-handed compliments to it. Continuity remained the order of the day, all the more so because American firms continued to extend their domination over both America and the world. Even with the introduction of the state firms, there was little turnover in the world's top two hundred companies until the 1970s. Obviously, Germany's and Japan's suicidal predilection for world domination made life much easier for America's commercial juggernauts after the Second World War. Yet, even within the American market, big firms continued to reap the rewards of organizational innovation.[16]

Between 1947 and 1968, the share of American corporate assets owned by the two hundred largest industrial companies rose steadily from 47.2 percent to 60.9 percent. Banks added branches and consolidated smaller divisions. Hotels, restaurants, rent-a-car services, spread their networks across the land, helped by the national highway system. The booming information-technology sector produced several new firms (such as Xerox, Texas Instruments, and Raytheon) that made it into the super league. But older firms hung around, too, such as General Telephone and Electric (GTE), Motorola, Clark Equipment, Honeywell, and, of course, IBM.[17]

As for oversight from Wall Street, the insurers, pension funds, and individual investors (whose numbers drifted down to 6 million in 1952 but then rose to 25 million by 1965) seemed happy to leave managers well enough alone. That may be because many of the shareholders were managers themselves, but dividend yields were taxed more harshly than capital gains. Rather than having to return their cash to their owners, postwar managers were free to invest it – thus making their firms even bigger and themselves even less reliant on shareholders to finance investment. About two-thirds of the almost $300 billion that nonfinancial companies raised between 1945 and 1970 came from internal sources.[18]

Firms also became, if anything, more bureaucratic and introspective. Decentralization became a job-creation machine for managers: by the 1960s, GE had amassed 190 separate departments, each with its own budget, and 43 strategic business units. The ubiquitous Peter Drucker temporarily shelved all his humanistic ideas about empowering workers to invent 'management by objectives,' an approach that dominated 'strategic thinking' for decades to come. In *The Practice of Management* (1954), he emphasized that both companies and managers needed clear objectives, and that the best way to achieve those objectives was to translate long-term strategy into short-term goals. In particular, he believed that a firm should have an elite group of general managers determining strategy and setting objectives for more specialized managers: 'Organization structure must be designed so as to make possible the achievement of the objectives of the business five, ten, fifteen years hence.'

ORGANIZATION MAN AND AMERICAN BENEVOLENCE

The security and predictability that American managers enjoyed in the 1950s and 1960s fostered something very akin to German stakeholder capitalism. Not only did companies enjoy close relations with the government ('What is good for General Motors is good for America'), they also spread their spoils among their various stakeholders. 'The job of management,' declared Frank Abrams, the chairman of Standard Oil of New Jersey, in a 1951 speech that was typical of the time, 'is to maintain an equitable and working balance among the claims of the various directly interested groups . . . stockholders, employees, customers, and the public at large.'[19] In *The New Industrial State* (1967), John Kenneth Galbraith argued that the United States was run by a quasi-benevolent oligopoly. A handful of big companies – the big three car companies and the big five steel companies, for example – planned the economy in the name of stability. They provided their blue-collar workers with lifetime employment and solid pensions, enjoyed fairly good relations with giant trade unions (around 40 percent of the workforce was unionized by 1960), and generally acted as good corporate citizens.

The most conspicuous beneficiaries were the managers. The 1950s and 1960s was the heyday of Company Man – or Organization Man, as he was then known.[20] He relished the traditions of office life: the assiduous secretaries (or office wives), the water cooler chatter, the convivial Christmas parties. He spent more time in the office than at home – which might well be situated in a bedroom suburb an hour's commute away – and often ended up leaving his wife for his secretary. He measured his life in terms of movement up the company hierarchy – a bigger office, a better parking space, a key to the executive washroom, and, finally, to cap it all, membership in the firm's quarter-century club.

Company Man's innate conformity began to worry a string of authors in the 1950s and 1960s. In *The Lonely Crowd* (1950), David Riesman noted that far too many Company Men were 'other directed' rather than 'inner directed' – more interested in the good opinion of their colleagues than in following their inner compass. In *The Organization Man* (1956), William H. Whyte worried that this emphasis on fitting in was stifling entrepreneurialism. (He quoted one IBM man proudly proclaiming that 'the training makes our men interchangeable.') In *The Status Seekers* (1959), Vance Packard showed how big companies devised intricate measures of status, from the size of offices to the horsepower of company cars – and how Company Men, like mice in some dismal scientific experiment, spent their lives scurrying around the treadmill and pressing the right buttons.

Yet, the mood among America's mice was still pretty triumphant. Their creed, after all, was being accepted well beyond the confines of Main Street. At home, America's bosses ran the government. Bob McNamara's Whiz Kids moved all too effortlessly from managing Ford to running the Vietnam War. Abroad, American companies conquered one European market after another. In a hugely popular book, *The American Challenge* (1968), Jean-Jacques Servan-Schreiber argued that the European Common Market (which was then in its ninth year) was basically an American organization. For this plucky Gallic resistance fighter, the problem was not America's financial power or technological brilliance: 'on the contrary, it is something quite new and considerably more serious – the extension to Europe of an organization that is still a mystery to us.'

'Mystery' was probably not quite the right word. The Europeans were determined to learn from the Americans. By 1970, more than half of Britain's hundred biggest industrial companies had turned to consultants from McKinsey to reorganize themselves; and a growing number of companies had adopted the multidivisional form that McKinsey and others championed. There were exceptions, of course, to accepting the American way, but they seemed only partial ones. Japanese and

German firms stuck to their more formal version of cooperative capitalism, but they also imported parts of the multidivisional structure; and their domestic economies were dominated by reassuringly big businesses.

The other element that underlined the supremacy of managerial capitalism was that the most conspicuous private-sector alternative to the multidivisional firm in the 1960s – the diversified conglomerate – was actually based on a slightly warped version of two Sloanist credos. Conglomerates like Gulf & Western ('Engulf & Devour') and ITT might have been cocky upstarts, driven by short-term stock-market gains rather than long-term planning. But, first, they believed that size mattered: that was one reason they kept on buying everything in sight. And, second, they were *über*-managerialists; their management skills, they believed, could master any sort of unrelated businesses, be it, in LTV's case, meatpacking and steel or, in Gulf & Western's, sugar refining and films.

The 1960s conglomerates arose partly by gobbling up the divisions that other companies did not want, and partly through hostile takeovers, often using their own highly rated shares. In both cases, they were helped by generous accounting rules and greedy investors (greedy not just for higher returns but also for something a bit more exciting than the steady growth of companies like GM). By 1973, fifteen of the top two hundred American manufacturing companies were conglomerates. But by then the bloom was off the rose. For all their frantic buying and selling, the conglomerates failed to deliver the returns shareholders expected. Shareholders consequently marked down their value, which in turn restricted their ability to take over more firms.

The Sloanist structure survived the assault fairly easily. But it should have heeded the warning. The manager-dominated company was in danger.

7   The Corporate Paradox
1975–2002

In 1973, the Sears Company proudly unveiled the world's tallest building. The skyscraper in downtown Chicago was a study in superlatives: 1,454 feet high, with 16,000 tinted windows and 80 miles of elevator cable. For Sears, it was a convenient bit of one-upmanship over Montgomery Ward. It was also a proclamation of the self-confidence of American capitalism. The American corporation bestrode the world. Why shouldn't it allow itself a little self-indulgence in the form of a 110-story tower?

Paradoxically, that self-confidence proved to be both eminently justified and hopelessly deluded. The justification was found in the triumph of private-sector capitalism, spurred on by privatization and deregulation around the world: the next twenty-five years saw the joint-stock company vastly expand its territory, trampling many of its rivals as it did so. The delusion was that it would be companies like Sears that would thrive in this freer world. By 2002, the basic idea of a big company – a multidivisional, hierarchical institution that could offer a lifetime career to its employees – had been unbundled. The increasing fragility of individual firms had profound effects on the company's relationship with the rest of society, with many of the doubts and frustrations bubbling to the surface after the Enron scandal in 2002.

HAIL THE COMPANY

In the early 1970s, big companies were expected to play a pivotal role in supporting the postwar consensus. In return for economic stability and social peace, they were expected to look after other stakeholders. But that consensus was beginning to get more burdensome. The economy in many countries was in a wretched state. Unions had seldom been more powerful: in 1974, the miners toppled Britain's Conserva-tive government. And even in America, governments kept introducing bother-some rules. In 1971, Richard Nixon introduced controls on wages and prices. His administration also launched affirmative action and established some of the coun-try's most powerful regulatory agencies, such as the Environmental Protection Agency and the Occupational Safety and Health Administra-tion.[1]

The deregulatory revolution began in Britain, where Margaret Thatcher was swept to power in 1979 by a wave of resentment over strikes and stagflation. Privatization was such a radical idea that the Tories scarcely mentioned it in their 1979 manifesto, and the government initially flirted with 'corporati-zation' – making public companies act more like private ones. Eventually, Thatcher and her guru, Keith Joseph, rejected the idea as insufficient – like trying to 'make a mule into a zebra by painting stripes down its back.'[2] The mules had to be put back in the private sector.

In 1982 and 1984, the government privatized its share in North Sea oil and gas; this was soon followed by British Telecom, British Gas, British Airways, and British Steel. Even the water supply and the electricity grid were handed over to private companies. By 1992, two-thirds of state-owned indus-tries had been pushed into the private sector. Privatization was invariably followed by the downsizing of the workforce (some-times by as much as 40 percent) and the upsizing of executive salaries, both of which raised the public's hackles, and the Con-servatives made a complete hash of privatizing British Rail. But in general the new companies improved the services on offer.

European governments soon followed suit, prompted by the introduction of the single market in 1992. Venerable national champions such as Volkswagen, Lufthansa, Renault, Elf Aquitaine, and ENI were wholly or partly privatized. Deutsche Telekom became Europe's largest privatization. In Latin America and Southeast Asia, government also sold off telecom companies and utilities, too often to their political supporters. But the most radical expansion of the company took place in the former Communist world.

In 1992, the Yeltsin government embarked on a gigantic program of privatization. It first 'corporatized' state-owned enterprises by rechartering them as joint-stock companies, with the state owning all the shares. It then issued vouchers to every Russian citizen (including children) to buy shares. By 1996, some eighteen thousand companies had been privatized, including more than three-quarters of all the larger industrial ones.[3] Even more than in Western Europe, this was far from an unqualified success: many of the new companies were still run by the old *nomenklatura*, and millions of people lost their jobs. Yet, some 40 million Russians became shareholders, and the idea of the company persisted.

The Chinese, by contrast, tiptoed into privatization. In the 1990s, they allowed small entrepreneurs to create companies. They also created a small class of 'red chips' – favored state firms that were allowed to register on the Hong Kong stock market. But at the Fifteenth Party Congress in 1997, the pace of reform increased dramatically. The Party decreed that most of the country's state companies – some of which employed thousands of people – would be freed from state control and operated as 'people-owned companies.' They would issue shares and be subjected to mergers and bankruptcy.

Meanwhile, the company expanded its range within its traditional hunting grounds. In Washington, D.C., too, the talk was of deregulation. Jimmy Carter started the ball rolling by deregulating the airline industry. Next came railroads and trucking. America's biggest regulated company, AT&T, was broken up in 1981. As we shall see, bureaucrats on both sides of the Atlantic were more ready than ever to circumscribe the activities of companies indirectly, adding social obligations. But even at the European Union they worked to make companies easier to set up: work began in Brussels on standardizing a European-wide company directive.

Meanwhile, within the existing private sector, the publicly quoted joint-stock company consolidated its hold over capitalism. There were still plenty of different sorts of businesses. Indeed, financiers and tax accountants conspired to invent new ones: open the back pages of any company's annual report in 2002 and you would find a lengthy list of 'single-purpose vehicles' and limited partnerships based in the Antilles (assuming such things were detailed at all, which, in some cases, notably Enron, they were not). But these were merely the outer defenses. In general, the larger businesses got, the more they tended to converge on the joint-stock idea. Around the world, institutions that had stuck to partnership structures or mutual societies for decades – Goldman Sachs, Lloyds of London, a whole host of insurers, friendly societies, and farmers' banks – converted to joint-stock companies.

THE UNBUNDLING OF THE COMPANY

Sears's perspective on the global triumph of the joint-stock company must have been mixed. Within a decade of the Sears tower appearing, America's biggest retailer was fighting for its independence. While Sears's managers had been going about their ancestral business of battling Montgomery Ward, the department-store market was disappearing, undermined partly by Wal-Mart, an upstart from Arkansas that Sears's internal positioning documents did not even mention until the 1980s. In 1992, Sam Walton (who incidentally had been offered a job by Sears as a young graduate from the University of Missouri back in 1940) died as America's richest retailer. In the same year, Sears made a net loss of $3.9 billion. A new chief executive, Arthur Martinez, saved the business only with the help of dramatic cutbacks. In 2001, a slimmed-down Sears announced that it was ceasing to be a department store: it would concentrate on clothes. As for Montgomery Ward, it had gone out of business in December 2000, laying off 37,000 people.

The rate at which large American companies left the *Fortune* 500 increased four times between 1970 and 1990. Names that once bespoke corporate permanence, like Pan Am or Barings Bank, disappeared. Corporate Icari, like Netscape and Enron (named the most innovative company in America by *Fortune* for six years in a row), emerged from nowhere and changed their industries but in one way or another flew too close to the sun and plummeted to the ground.

Far from being a source of comfort, bigness became a code for inflexibility, the antithesis of the new credo, entrepreneurialism. In 1974, America's one hundred biggest industrial companies accounted for 35.8 percent of the country's gross domestic product; by 1998, that figure had fallen to 17.3 percent. Their share of the nation's workforce and its corporate assets also roughly halved.[4] Big firms grew (by 1999, the average revenue of the top fifty companies in America reached $51 billion); they just grew much more slowly than small ones, which supplied most of the new jobs throughout the developed world. Big firms were much more likely than ever to go out of business: by 2000, roughly half the biggest one hundred industrial firms in 1974 had disappeared through take-overs or bankruptcy.[5]

The big firms that survived this maelstrom only did so by dint of bloody internal revolutions. In the first five years of the 1990s, IBM, a company once so stable that it refused to sack people during the Depression, laid off 122,000 of its workers, roughly a quarter of the total. Jack Welch's two-decade reign at General Electric began in the 1980s with a period of shocking corporate brutality. A series of quasi-Maoist revolutions followed, complete with slogans (Work Out, Six Sigma, Destroyyourbusiness.com) and methods (getting thousands of managers to measure each other's 'boundarylessness,' and sacking the underperformers). By the time Welch retired in 2002, GE, which had repeatedly been voted the world's most admired company, had become at its heart a services conglomerate. Despite this painful metamorphosis, the company still looked vulnerable, with analysts wondering whether Welch's successor could keep the group together.

By the turn of the millennium, it no longer seemed odd that, at least for a time, the biggest challenge to the world's richest man, Bill Gates, should suddenly spring up in a Finnish university dorm or that its product – the new operating system, Linux – should be given away for free. Such uncertainty proved too much for the Sloanist idea of a company. It was too slow, too methodical, too hierarchical, too reliant on economies of scale that were withering away. It also proved too cumbersome when it came to husbanding knowledge.

Brainpower had always mattered in business. But this truism became far more valid after 1975, as Peter Drucker's knowledge workers finally began to make their weight felt. By the end of

2001, General Motors boasted net-book assets (tangible things like factories, cars, and even cash) of $52 billion, but its market value of $30 billion was only a fifth of that of Merck, a drug firm that could muster a balance sheet value of $7 billion, but had a far more valuable trove of knowledge. In 1999, America's most valuable export was intellectual capital: the country raked in $37 billion in licensing fees and royalties, compared with $29 billion for its main physical export, aircraft.[6]

The story of the company in the last quarter of the twentieth century is of a structure being unbundled. Companies were gradually forced to focus on their 'core competencies.' Ronald Coase's requirement of the company – it had to do things more efficiently than the open market – was being much more sorely tested.

The managers of big companies liked to claim that new technology made it more efficient to bundle things together in a single company. In a few cases, this proved correct. Big media conglomerates were able to sell the same 'content' through different channels. New technology to monitor drivers in the trucking industry in the 1980s made it cheaper for shippers to employ them directly, so they got bigger.[7]

Yet, for the most part, the world was moving in the opposite direction. Despite all the consolidation at the top of the media world, the number of small companies in places like Hollywood multiplied, with many of these specialists sucking most of the value out of the industry. More people left big firms to set up on their own: in Britain, for instance, the number of companies rose by 50 percent between 1980 and 1996.[8] And as big companies were forced to refocus on the things that they could do cheaper or better than outsiders, they discovered that such 'core competencies' lay not in tangible things, such as factory equipment, but in intangible values: the culture of discovery at Glaxo

Wellcome, for instance, or the traditions of engineering at Mercedes-Benz.

It is perhaps not surprising that hollowing out was commonplace in Silicon Valley: Cisco managed to become one of America's biggest manufacturers while only directly making a quarter of the products it sold. But the same thing was also happening in older firms. For instance, Ford's River Rouge plant in Dearborn, Michigan, had once represented the zenith of integration, employing 100,000 workers to make twelve hundred cars a day, and producing almost everything itself, including its steel. Yet, by 2001, 3,000 people at River Rouge produced eight hundred Mustangs a day, mainly assembling parts sent in by outsiders, and Ford's bosses were talking about the carmaker becoming a 'vehicle brand owner,' which would design, engineer, and market cars, but not actually make them.[9]

ROUND UP THE USUAL SUSPECTS

There was something strangely backward-looking about all this. The networks of specialists, the ever-changing alliances, the constant sense of foreboding: these might have been familiar to the Merchant of Prato.

Three groups of people played a leading role in unbundling the corporation: the Japanese, Wall Street, and Silicon Valley. The creativity, carnage, and (sometimes) corruption that this trio unleashed in turn set the scene for a fourth player to reassert itself in the wake of the Enron scandal: the government.

In the mid-1950s, a young Londoner with a taste for the open road and the wind on his face would never have dreamed of looking beyond Britain to buy a motorbike. What could be more stylish than a Vincent Black Shadow, a Triumph Thunderbird, or a Norton Dominator? Harley-Davidson commanded similar feudal loyalty from Americans. A decade later, bikers everywhere were aware of an alternative. At first, the main attraction of Honda, Yamaha, Kawasaki, and Suzuki was price. But the four Japanese firms soon became the industry's pioneers, introducing electric starters, four-cylinder engines, and five-speed transmissions, and launching new models every year. By 1981, Harley-Davidson had been forced to seek government protection, and the British motorcycle industry was to all intents and purposes dead.

This story seemed emblematic. In 1980, Chrysler, obliterated by better Japanese cars, lost $1.7 billion and had to be bailed out by the government. Sony and Matsushita had sewn up the consumer-electronics industry, and the Japanese had Silicon Valley on the run. Meanwhile, the idea that Japanese capitalism could work only with Japanese workers was about to be shattered. During the 1980s, the Japanese made direct investments overseas of $280 billion, ten times the figure for the previous three decades.[10] That still left Japanese companies with a smaller share of corporate America than the British, and a much smaller share of corporate Europe than the Americans.[11] But their change in stature was dramatic. They picked up a string of corporate trophies, including Firestone, Columbia Pictures, Rockefeller Center, and two of the world's best golf courses, Turnberry and Pebble Beach.

In 1992, *Rising Sun* surged to the top of the best-seller lists: its author, Michael Crichton, painted a picture of a fiendish master race of businessmen, marshaled into families of firms and backed by an inscrutable government, cannily outmaneuvering their naïve American peers. This view was hardly confined to cheap novels. In the early 1990s, the business sections of American bookstores were crammed with paeans to Japanese capitalism. In Europe, the myth of the unstoppable Japanese company neatly replaced the 1960s myth of the unstoppable American company. Japanese manufacturers reinvented the once-reviled British car industry, turning allegedly work-shy Geordies into paragons of productivity – and creating what one French car boss unsubtly dubbed 'an off-shore aircraft carrier' to attack the Continent.

Of course, Crichton was wrong. In the eight years following the publication of *Rising Sun*, the Nikkei index lost around two-thirds of its value, while the NASDAQ, reflecting those battered American high technologists, rose fivefold. The Japanese model of the company proved to have its problems. Yet it still managed to change business around the world, not least because it represented a cohesive alternative to the Western model.[12]

At the heart of the Japanese model was Toyota's system of lean production. After the war, Toyota's bosses toured American factories and became obsessed by the amount of *muda* or wasted effort they saw. They turned to the ideas not only of Peter Drucker but also of W. Edwards Deming (1900–1993), who focused on improving quality. (Deming was virtually unknown in America; by 1950, Japan had a much-publicized annual Deming Prize for manufacturing excellence.) Toyota treated all the different parts of the production system – development, purchasing, manufacturing – as a seamless process, rather than a series of separate departments. It brought together several important ideas, such as total quality management (putting every worker in charge of the quality of products), continuous improvement (getting those workers to suggest improvements), and just-in-time manufacturing (making sure that parts get to factories only when they are needed). Workers were put into self-governing teams, and there was far more contact with suppliers.

These ideas were shocking to American managers. Under the Sloanist system, 'quality control' was a department. The idea of allowing a worker to stop a production line seemed heretical. Indeed, many American companies initially missed the point, and decided that Japan's success was based on technology: General Motors, for instance, spent billions on robots in a desperate attempt to catch up with Toyota. But gradually they began to learn from the Japanese. In 1987, America launched its own equivalent of the Deming Prize, the Baldrige. America's high-tech industries discovered that as long as they embraced Japanese manufacturing methods, they could compete in innovation and design. Harley-Davidson used its period under government protection to change its working practices as well as to upgrade its machinery. By the early 1990s, it was back on level terms with its Japanese peers.

The other part of the Japanese model might be dubbed 'long-termism.' Japanese companies believed in lifetime employment for all (something that their Western rivals tended to reserve for white-collar workers). Management was usually by consensus – again something Jack Welch would have found inconceivable. Japanese companies operated in families or *keiretsu* – reinventing the *zaibatsu* that General MacArthur had broken up – while American companies operated as independent units. And while Western companies tended to be accountable to short-term investors, Japanese firms financed their expansion with loans from their *keiretsu* banks. As for profits, these were deemed less important than market share. Japanese firms were prepared to tolerate very low returns on investment. And they had the firm support of the Japanese government, which protected some of the weaker *keiretsu* industries, and also turned a blind eye both to corporate-governance questions and to antitrust considerations.

In the late 1980s, this 'long-term' stakeholder capitalism represented a real challenge to shareholder capitalism – not least because critics could also point to other apparent successes. South Korea's *chaebol*, which had broadly copied the *keiretsu* system, were seen as the next threat. German companies were outperforming their Anglo-American peers in some high-profile industries, notably luxury cars. They, too, were protected from the distractions of short-term capitalism by their two-tier board systems, the argument went; they, too, ruled through consensus and works councils rather than through strikes and layoffs; they, too, enjoyed government support, rather than being left to sink or swim.

In the 1990s, admiration gave way to doubt. There were several reasons why Japan stagnated, not least macroeconomic mismanagement, but the stakeholder ideal was one of them. Consensus management often became an excuse for paralysis; lifetime employment not only proved impossible to maintain but also was a formidable barrier to promoting young talent. Clever young Japanese bankers and businesspeople migrated to Western firms that were prepared to give them more responsibility, not to mention money. *Keiretsu* firms tended to overproduce and overinvest when compared with independent firms. Even in the boom years of 1971 to 1982, they derived significantly lower returns on assets.[13] In the 1990s, they drifted from one disaster to another.

The decade was also a humbling one both for the *chaebol*, which were flattened by the Asian currency crisis and charges of crony capitalism, and for German companies, which were hamstrung by the high labor costs that stakeholder capitalism entailed. The relative absence of 'short-term' shareholder pressure proved a comparative weakness – all the more so because Anglo-Saxon firms, particularly American ones, were just beginning to benefit from genuine investor pressure.

BARBARIANS AND PENSION FUNDS

In the heyday of managerial capitalism, 'shareholder activism' was limited to cases so extreme that they made a nonsense of the term, such as the occasion in 1955 when City of London institutions forced the dictatorial Sir Bernard Docker out of BSA/Daimler, after a series of revelations about his luxurious lifestyle, including Lady Docker's frequent use of a bespoke gold-plated Daimler. The only real option open to unhappy shareholders was to do 'the Wall Street shuffle' – to sell the shares and look elsewhere.

This comfortable state of affairs relied on shareholders remaining both dispersed and submissive. But over the next quarter of a century, the power of big investment institutions rose relentlessly: by 1980, they owned a third of the shares on Wall Street; by 2000, more than 60 percent. Pension funds grew particularly fast – from 0.8 percent of the market in 1950 to more than 30 percent by the end of the century. This handed enormous power to organizations such as the huge California Public Employees Retirement System. ('Guys,' the treasurer of California remarked to his peers in New Jersey and New York, whom he had summoned to a hotel room in 1984 during an oil battle, 'in this room we control the future of Phillips. All we have to do is vote the proxy.')[14]

It was not just a question of numbers, but of status. Here mutual funds, which also grew quickly (from 2 percent of the market in 1950 to 12 percent in 1994), and various savings schemes launched by governments, such as ISAs and PEPs in

Britain and 401k plans in America, were crucial, because they forced savers to start checking up on investment managers and their quarterly performance figures. From being rather dowdy creatures, fund managers became downright glamorous, their bespectacled faces peering owlishly from the front of magazines, their words of wisdom captivating the masses on CNBC. Peter Lynch, who built Fidelity's Magellan Fund into the largest in the market, became better known than the corporate managers whom he backed – and occasionally sacked.

Fund managers were quick to dump shares in order to boost their quarterly earnings, a habit that helped drive up volume on the New York Stock Exchange from 962 million shares in 1962 to 27.5 billion in 1985 and 262 billion in 2000. But they were also more likely to interfere in the companies they owned. For a huge institution like Calpers, it was not easy to off-load the 7.2 million shares it owned in General Motors; when the company began to lose billions in the early 1990s, Calpers called for heads to roll. In 1992, GM's board ousted its slow-moving chief executive, Roger Stempel (the first such coup since Pierre du Pont got rid of Durant seventy years earlier). Stempel was soon followed by his peers at IBM, Westinghouse, American Express, and Kodak.

Meanwhile, the investment world became infinitely more complex, as markets deregulated and computers popped up in dealing rooms. The development in the 1960s of the offshore 'euromarket' in London prompted more flexible rules in New York, which in turn prompted more flexible rules everywhere else. By the early 1980s, the Western world had an integrated foreign exchange market and, for big firms at least, a global bond market. Soon mathematicians were dreaming up ever more ingenious forms of swaps, options, and other derivatives. The first hedge funds appeared, while other phrases such as 'off balance sheet liabilities' acquired new meanings.

Yet, the Wall Street figures who struck most fear into managers were the corporate raiders – particularly now that they focused on using debt to dismantle companies. One of the pioneers was Hanson Trust, a British conglomerate that did half its deals in America. Set up in 1964 by two buccaneering Yorkshiremen, James Hanson and Gordon White, it rose to prominence in the 1970s by taking over a series of unglamorous but cash-rich businesses, such as brick firms and tobacco firms. Once a takeover had been completed, Hanson rapidly repaid some of the debt by selling assets (typically a now-unnecessary head office) and then set about pruning management. Any acquired business was theoretically up for sale almost immediately: Hanson was rather like an antique dealer, buying slightly dingy assets, polishing them up, and putting them back in the shop window.

Most of the other raiders also had a sense of swagger. T. Boone Pickens was a folksy oilman who found that he could make a fortune by failing to take over oil firms: thanks to the rising share price, he made $500 million in one foray at Gulf alone. Carl Icahn, a former stock-market trader who liked to pontificate about the way that 'the corporate welfare state' was smothering the American economy, bought TWA. The most beguiling of all was Sir James Goldsmith (1933–1997). Having made several hundred million dollars asset-stripping Diamond International, a timber firm, he bought 11.5 percent of Goodyear in 1986. The tire company's hometown, Akron, Ohio, responded furiously. A subsequent congressional hearing was dominated by a broadside by Goldsmith against the corrupting effect of entrenched management, but he eventually retreated, selling his shares at a profit of $93 million.

The battle that came to define the 1980s takeover boom

occurred in 1988. RJR Nabisco was formed by the marriage, in 1985, of the Reynolds tobacco business and Nabisco Brands. But the stock market was unimpressed by the union, and the firm's high-spending chief executive, Ross Johnson, began to talk to Wall Street about taking the company private. He chose Shearson Lehman, part of American Express, to advise him; but after a fierce battle, the company was eventually bought by Kohlberg Kravis Roberts, an adviser whom Johnson had somewhat foolishly spurned, for $25 billion. Johnson was given a $53 million payoff; thousands of his former workers lost their jobs in the subsequent rationalization.

KKR was a new sort of organization – a leveraged buyout partnership that created a succession of investment funds. Formed in 1976 by three bankers from Bear Stearns, KKR had already taken over Beatrice Foods (in an $8.7 billion buyout) and Safeway ($4.8 billion) and a string of smaller firms. The structures varied, but KKR's fund put in a relatively small portion of equity – in RJR's case, only $1.5 billion. Following the same sort of procedures as Hanson, it then paid off the debt, ideally leaving the equity-holders sitting on an enormous profit.

At heart, leveraged buyouts were an attempt to make managers think like owners. In 1989, Michael Jensen of the Harvard Business School claimed that such private firms heralded the 'eclipse of the public corporation,' because they resolved the conflict between owners and managers in a much clearer way. He heralded debt as a more demanding way of financing companies than equity: 'Equity is soft, debt hard. Equity is forgiving, debt insistent. Equity is a pillow, debt is a sword.'[15]

In fact, the success rate of leveraged buyouts depended enormously on the price that was paid. The main winners were usually the original shareholders, who sold tired-looking companies at massive premiums: the price KKR paid for Safeway was 82 percent above its market value three months before. Buyouts were less popular with unions, who associated them with large redundancies. This was unfair: the seventeen companies bought out by KKR in 1977–1989 increased employment by 310,000 (and also spent more on research and development).[16] But the process could be savage. At Safeway, for instance, where the company motto had been 'Safeway offers security,' 63,000 people lost their jobs.[17]

LBOs, in turn, relied on another Wall Street invention: 'junk bonds.' Wall Street had always traded bonds in distressed companies. The genius of Michael Milken was to create bonds specifically for this 'non-investment-grade' market, opening up the market to ventures that were too small or risky to issue regular bonds. Milken first began to push his 'high-yield' bonds in the 1970s; by the 1980s, his firm, Drexel Burnham Lambert, dominated the junk-bond market, and his annual Predators Ball in Los Angeles had become a fixture for entrepreneurs and politicians. In 1982, President Reagan made Milken's job a little easier by allowing banks and, crucially, savings and loan institutions to buy corporate bonds. Between 1975 and 1986, some $71.5 billion of junk bonds were issued, with an average yield of 13.6 percent.

In some ways, the merger boom ended in disaster. Junk bonds lived up to their name: around a fifth of the bonds issued from 1978 to 1983 had defaulted by 1988.[18] Many of the thrifts that bought junk bonds went bankrupt, as did Drexel Burnham Lambert itself in February 1990. Milken was indicted on almost one hundred counts of racketeering – and eventually sent to jail. Across in Britain, Hanson's ambition overran itself: after an unsuccessful play for ICI, its two founders effectively broke up the company in 1996. Goldsmith ended his career as an antiglobalization crusader. Wall Streeters were pilloried for their greed in *The Bonfire of the Vanities* (1987), *Liar's Poker* (1989), and *Barbarians at the Gate* (1991).

By the end of the century, shareholders had plainly failed to restrain managerial power in the way that many had hoped. Nine in ten big American companies were incorporated in Delaware, a state whose laws favored managers over shareholders. The experiment of making managers behave more like owners had been perverted, via excessive use of stock options, into a get-rich-quick scheme for bosses. By the end of the 1990s, the chief executives of big companies took home an average of $12.4 million – six times as much as in 1990.[19] A couple of years later, the Enron scandal revealed managerial abuses on a scale that the staid Company Men of the 1950s could never have imagined. Hostile takeovers were far rarer in continental Europe and Japan and companies' managers were much better protected by their close ties to banks.

Still, these qualifications should not obscure how much the 1980s merger boom changed companies. LBOs, for instance, did not go away: indeed, the device spread to Europe and eventually Japan. Many of the management techniques pioneered by LBO funds, such as incentivizing managers with stakes in their businesses, spread widely. As for takeovers, ten years after the world gawked with disbelief at the size of the RJR Nabisco deal, three takeovers trebled the amount: Glaxo Wellcome bought SmithKline Beecham for $76 billion, Pfizer paid $85 billion for Warner Lambert, and Exxon paid $77 billion for Mobil. In 2000, Vodafone, a British mobile phone company, stunned the German establishment by winning control of Mannesmann in a hostile takeover. And the power of investment managers continued to grow. By 2002, three groups – Fidelity, the Union Bank of Switzerland, and Allianz – each controlled about $1 trillion in assets.

These investors were far from omnipotent, as Enron showed. Yet, with the barbarians and pension funds at the gate, company managers were continuously reminded of the aphorism 'Money goes where it wants and stays where it is well treated.' Companies had to ask hard questions about their scope. Investors, with a few prominent exceptions, wanted companies to be good at one thing: diversification was something they could do themselves. And they were remorseless about punishing bureaucratic flab. It was no coincidence that the main corporate heroes of the period all hailed from a place famous for small, agile firms – the thin sliver of land between San Jose and San Francisco that had once been known as the Valley of Heart's Delight.

SILICON VALLEY

In 1996, with the Internet revolution gathering pace, John Perry Barlow, a Grateful Dead songwriter and cyber guru, issued the following warning: 'Governments of the Industrial World, you weary giants of flesh and steel, I come from Cyberspace, the new home of the Mind. I ask you of the past to leave us alone. You are not welcome among us.' Silicon Valley's penchant for hyperbole can be grating. All the same, the business ideas that the Valley pioneered, combined with the technology it invented, helped unbundle the company still further.

Silicon Valley's story actually dates back to 1938, when David Packard and a fellow Stanford engineering student, Bill Hewlett, set up shop in a garage in Palo Alto. In the 1950s, Hewlett-Packard, along with several other Stanford-inspired companies, moved into the university's new industrial park. Over the next two decades, this cluster of small firms multiplied slowly with plenty of help from the government. By one count, in the period 1958 to 1974, the Pentagon paid for $1 billion worth of semiconductor research. Packard served as deputy secretary of defense in the first Nixon administration.

In the 1970s, the Valley began to acquire its identity. The name 'Silicon Valley' was invented in 1971 by a local technology journalist – reflecting the success of its memory-chip makers. Meanwhile, the Valley began to be taken over by the sort of people who protested against the Vietnam War, rather than helped run it. In 1976, Steve Jobs and Steve Wozniak set up Apple Computer in the Jobs family garage. But the 1970s boom was brought to a halt by the Japanese. On 'the black day,' March 28, 1980, Richard Anderson, a HP manager, revealed that tests had shown the Japanese memory chips outperformed the Valley's. To its shame, the Valley turned to the American government for protection, but it also successfully changed shape, outsourcing its manufacturing and diversifying from chips into computer software.

This metamorphosis underlined what set the Valley apart.[20] America's other high-tech center, Boston's Route 128, boasted just as much venture capital, and just as many universities. Yet, when both clusters fell from grace in the mid-1980s, Silicon Valley proved far more resilient. The reason was structural. Big East Coast firms such as Digital Equipment and Data General were self-contained empires that focused on one product, minicomputers. Silicon Valley's network of small firms endlessly spawned new ones.

It was for much the same reason that the Internet business found a natural home in northern California. The late 1990s saw an unprecedented number of young Valley firms going public. In 2000 alone, some $20 billion of venture capital was pumped into the region. By then, the Internet bubble was already bursting. Even allowing for that (and all the Valley's other drawbacks, such as high house prices, terrible traffic, and unrelenting ugliness), the region still counted as the most dynamic industry cluster in the world. By 2001, Silicon Valley provided jobs for 1.35 million people, roughly three times the figure for 1975, its productivity and income levels were roughly double the national averages, and it collected one in twelve new patents in America.[21]

Silicon Valley changed companies in two ways. The first was through the products it made. At the heart of nearly all of them was the principle of miniaturization. In the last three decades of the twentieth century, the cost of computing processing power tumbled by 99.99 percent – or 35 percent a year.[22] Computers thrust ever more power down the corporate hierarchy – to local area networks, to the desktop, and increasingly to outside the office altogether. Meanwhile, the Internet reduced transaction costs. By the end of the century, General Electric and Cisco were forcing their suppliers to bid for their business in on-line auctions; and eBay, the main independent on-line auction house, had 42 million users around the world. In the last three months of 2001, those eBay customers listed 126 million items and spent \$2.7 billion. Previously, those transactions, if they had happened at all, would have involved thousands of intermediaries.

The other way in which Silicon Valley changed the company was by pioneering an alternative form of corporate life. Some of its companies, such as Hewlett-Packard and Intel, lasted for decades, but the Valley epitomized the idea of 'creative destruction.' An unusual amount of the Valley's growth came from gazelle companies – firms whose sales had grown by at least 20 percent in each of the previous four years. It also tolerated failure and even treachery to an unusual degree. Many would argue that its real birth date was not 1938 but the moment in

1957 when the so-called 'traitorous eight' walked out of Shockley Laboratories to found Fairchild Semiconductor, which in turn spawned Intel and another thirty-six firms. Virtually every big firm in Silicon Valley was a spin-off from another one.

Right from the beginning, it was a place where ties were optional, and first names compulsory. In 1956, the same year that *The Organization Man* was published, William Shockley (1910–1989) took all his colleagues out to breakfast in Palo Alto to celebrate the fact that he had won the Nobel Prize for inventing the transistor: a photograph shows only two of them wearing ties, and nobody wearing a suit.[23] Meritocracy was crucial: youth was promoted on ability alone, and the Valley was unusually open to immigrants. In 2001, one resident in three was foreign-born.

By the end of the twentieth century, you could see the gradual Siliconization of commerce. The hierarchies of big firms everywhere became looser. Manpower, a temporary worker agency, replaced General Motors as America's biggest employer. Most economies relied on gazelle firms to produce jobs (by some counts, they provided three-quarters of the new jobs in the mid-1990s). Firms everywhere discovered the benefits of alliances, partnerships, joint ventures, and franchises. By one estimate, around a fifth of the revenues of America's biggest one thousand companies in 1997 came from alliances of one sort or another. The border of the company, so rigidly defined under Alfred Sloan, became fuzzy – or, in the jargon of the time, 'virtual.'

As the previously firm lines around companies began to blur, some old business ideas began to seem extremely modern. Business experts like Michael Porter pointed to the competitive advantages buried in the guildlike networks of German engineering firms. East Asia, the most exciting area of business geographically, was dominated by 'bamboo networks' of overseas Chinese companies. Rather than trying to set up state companies, governments were now fixated by trying to foster entrepreneurial clusters of their own in places as far apart as the South of France, Malaysia, and Taiwan.

UNBUNDLED, FLAT, AND BORDERLESS

To ascribe everything that happened to the company in the final quarter of the twentieth century to Silicon Valley, Wall Street, and the Japanese would be an oversimplification. But this trio provided the discordant background music to a period of mounting uncertainty.

Nothing better symbolized the loss of confidence than the rise of the management-theory industry. As companies rushed to outsource everything in sight, many even outsourced their thinking to a growing number of 'witch doctors.' By 2000, McKinsey had four thousand consultants, ten times the number in 1975. Other companies – notably IT firms and accountants – established consulting businesses. The accountants at Arthur Andersen were so jealous of the fees being charged by their colleagues at Andersen Consulting that they tried to invade the business themselves, a move that led to one of the most expensive divorces in corporate history. This was a time when fads such as business-process reengineering sped around the world at a dizzying pace, and when businesspeople rushed to buy books that distilled the management wisdom of Siegfried and Roy, the English rugby captain, *Star Trek*, and Jesus, CEO.

As the company jumped through these hoops, its relationship with the rest of society changed again. By the 1990s, companies had begun to move their headquarters out of city centers. Rather than displaying their might to the world, they preferred to retreat into low-slung business campuses in the suburbs. The cult of the bottom line was forcing companies to do away with what their bosses deemed to be unnecessary expenditure, even if it meant abandoning their old civic responsibilities.

Philadelphia, which had done so well out of the robber barons, got clobbered. Scott Paper had been a pillar of civic life in Philadelphia for decades. But in 1993 it posted a loss, and in 1994 it brought in Al Dunlap to boost its flagging performance. 'Chainsaw Al' moved the headquarters to Florida, laid off thousands of workers, reneged on a promise to pay the final $50,000 of a $250,000 pledge to the Philadelphia Museum of Art, and finally sold the business to Kimberly-Clark.[24] Another staple of local civic life, Drexel and Company, wound up as part of Drexel Burnham Lambert, and was forced out of business by federal prosecutors. SmithKline merged with a British company, Beecham.[25] Meanwhile, many of Philadelphia's new companies preferred the anonymity of Route 202 to the expensive amenities of downtown.

For Company Man, the period was brutal. All his basic values were under assault – loyalty, malleability, and willingness to put in face time. The new hero of the business world was the tieless entrepreneur rather than the man in the gray-flannel suit. Women began to provide competition, not just secretarial assistance. Jack Welch complained that lifetime employment produced a 'paternal, feudal, fuzzy kind of loyalty' – and forced his employees to compete to keep their jobs.[26] In IBM towns, like Endicott and Armonk, IBM men lost more than their jobs; they lost access to the cocoon of institutions, such as the IBM country club, with which the company had long protected them.

This devastation can be exaggerated. Some company towns,

such as Redmond, boomed during the period. In Delaware, Du Pont may have faded (its workforce was slashed from 25,000 to 9,000), but its role in local society was partly assumed by MBNA, an uppity credit-card firm that employed 10,500 people in the state by 2002.[27] Company Man did not so much die as enroll in a witness-protection program. Successful companies usually possessed powerful corporate cultures – something that are impossible to maintain without a hard core of loyal employees. Under Welch, General Electric might not have believed in lifetime employment, but it certainly hired a distinct brand of person wherever it went (broadly, a competitive male, with a keen interest in sports, usually from a second-tier university). The Microserfs in Redmond may not have worn blue suits, like IBM's foot soldiers, but they still boasted a strong clannish spirit.

As for the much mooted death of the career, the aggregate statistics suggest that workers in the 1990s were changing their jobs only slightly more frequently than they did in the 1970s.[28] The biggest novelty was the sharp rise in temporary jobs for women. With the possible exception of Britain, where almost a quarter of the workforce was part-time, it would be hard to make the case that the job was disappearing; and even harder to make the case that workers wanted it to disappear.[29] The biggest change was psychological: even if people were continuing to work at companies, the old certainties of employment and position had patently gone. People talked about employability, not lifetime employment. Career paths followed a more topsy-turvy route; and everyone began to work longer hours. Sociologists such as Richard Sennett (*The Corrosion of Character*, 1998) worried about the growth of anxiety even in those people who had done well in the system.

REGULATORY CAPITALISM

These changes began to pose questions about the company's relationship with the state. By 2002, society's attitude toward the corporate sector seemed two-faced. On the one hand, governments had set the company free, deregulating markets, loosening trade barriers, and privatizing state-owned companies. On the other hand, politicians and pressure groups were looking for ways to turn the company to social ends.

Many governments had given up power reluctantly anyway. The French, for instance, carefully rigged their privatizations so that they could preserve as much state planning as possible, selling packages of shares to friendly strategic investors. They thought nothing of introducing a thirty-five-hour week in 2000. Throughout the 1990s, European governments, both individually and through the European Union, increased red tape dramatically in the name of the common good. Consumers had to be protected, safety standards had to be met, and products (including, famously, the banana) had to be defined. According to the British government's own regulatory impact assessments, the European working-time directive alone, which set a maximum forty-eight-hour week, was costing the country's businesses more than £2 billion a year by 2001.[30] According to the same figures, Tony Blair's Labour government had added £15 billion worth of regulatory costs in its first five years.

The American government also increased its grip on the company through laws governing health, safety, the environment, employee and consumer rights, and affirmative action. Often the effect was not just more red tape but also more lawsuits. The 1991 Civil Rights Act, signed by George Bush senior, imposed huge regulatory burdens on businesses. It also created a litigation bonanza by increasing attorneys' fees and allowing claims for 'emotional injury.' American managers were more restricted than ever before in performing one of their most basic functions – hiring and firing. They could not ask about such things as an applicant's family or his health. Bill Clinton was a still more fervent micromanager. By the end of the century, the cost of meeting social regulations to American firms was $289 billion a year, according to the Office of Management and Budget, a figure that other ex-perts reckon was only a third of the real amount.[31] And there were other 'costs' to America – particularly the ever-growing amount of time that companies put into political lobbying (both in Washington, D.C., and in various state capitals) to twist this sprawling thicket of rules to their own advantage.

Meanwhile, both the British and American governments began to niggle away at one of the tenets of 'Anglo-Saxon' shareholder capitalism: the idea that companies should be run for their shareholders. During the 1980s, about half of America's fifty states introduced laws that allowed managers to consider other stakeholders alongside shareholders. Connecticut even introduced a law that required them to do so. In Britain, the 1985 Companies Act took the same approach, forcing directors to consider the interests of employees as well as shareholders.

If the main thrust of regulatory capitalism was social, there was also a corporate-governance element as well. Worried by the buccaneering spirit that deregulation had unleashed and by the piratical excesses of some corporate captains, governments sporadically tried to call the bosses of companies more firmly to account. In some cases, regulators breached the corporate veil – holding directors personally responsible for their firms' actions. In Britain, for instance, the 1986 Insolvency Act made directors liable for the debts a company incurred after the point when they might reasonably be expected to have closed it down. But the real onslaught occurred in America, after the New Economy bubble burst.

ENRON AND BEYOND

The 1990s was a decade of infatuation with companies. The number of magazines devoted to business multiplied, even as the ages of the smiling chief executives on their covers plummeted. But the adoration went well beyond young whippersnappers. When Roberto Goizueta, the veteran boss of Coca-Cola, tried to justify his $80 million pay packet to a share-holder meeting, he was interrupted four times – with applause. It was thus hardly surprising that, in January 2001, the new administration tried to capitalize on the prevail-ing probusiness mood by presenting George W. Bush as America's first M.B.A. president; nor that he stuffed his cabinet with chief executives; nor even that he pursued a shamelessly probusiness policy, allowing companies to help craft a new national energy policy and hinting at repeal of some of Bill Clinton's social regulation.

A year and a half later, everything had changed. By the summer of 2002, Bush had signed into law the Sarbanes-Oxley Act, arguably the toughest piece of corporate legislation since the 1930s. Meanwhile, many of the bosses who had once graced business covers were now facing criminal charges. The American people were furious: 70 percent of them said that they did not trust what their brokers or corporations told them and 60 percent called corporate wrongdoing 'a widespread problem.'[32] Even bosses who had not been caught doing anything wrong, such as Hank Paulson of Goldman Sachs and Andy Grove of Intel, felt obliged to apologize to the public for the sorry state of American capitalism.[33] Meanwhile, in continental Europe, the two bosses who had most obviously proclaimed themselves dis-ciples of the Ameri-can way – Thomas Middelhoff of Germany's Bertelsmann and Jean-Marie Messier of France's Vivendi – were both sacked.

The general catalyst for this revolution was the burst-ing of America's stock-market bubble. Between March 2000 and July 2002, this destroyed $7 trillion in wealth – a sum equivalent to a quarter of the financial assets owned by Americans (and an eighth of their total wealth). The spread of mutual funds and the change from defined-benefit to defined-contribution retirement plans meant that this was a truly democratic crash: most of the households in America lost money directly.

The specific catalyst was, ironically enough, one of the firms that Bush had turned to to design his energy policy. Enron was a darling of the 1990s – a new form of energy company that did not rely on drilling and gas stations but on teams of financial traders. A Harvard Business School case study was approvingly titled 'Enron's Transformation: From Gas Pipelines to New Economy Powerhouse.'

Unfortunately, the energy trading company took its pen-chant for innovation just a little too far. Its managers used highly complicated financial engineering – convoluted partner-ships, off-the-books debt, and exotic hedging techniques – to hide huge losses. And when those losses emerged, they sold mil-lions in company stock while their employees were prohibited from doing likewise. All the corporate overseers who were employed to monitor Enron on behalf of its shareholders – the outside directors, auditors, regulators, and stockbroking ana-lysts – were found wanting. Despite four centuries of corporate advancement, the hapless shareholders turned out to be no better protected or informed than the London merchants who dispatched Edward Fenton to the East Indies in 1582, only to see him head off to St. Helena, hoping to declare himself king.

Enron's collapse led to the destruction of Arthur Andersen, a giant accounting firm that had signed off on its books (and had also made a mint providing consulting advice). The government charged Andersen with obstructing justice by willfully destroying Enron documents. Soon afterward, WorldCom followed. The telecom giant, it emerged, had perpetrated one of the most sweeping (and crude) bookkeeping deceptions in corporate history, overstating a key measure of earnings by more than $3.8 billion over five quarters, starting in January 2001. Meanwhile, its boss, Bernard Ebbers, had apparently treated the company as a piggy bank, borrowing hundreds of millions of dollars when it suited him. WorldCom's stock, which peaked at $64.50 in 1999, stopped trading at 83 cents, costing investors about $175 billion – nearly three times what was lost in the implosion of Enron.

A stream of other scandals followed: Xerox and AOL Time Warner had to revise their accounts. The former boss of Tyco, who had taken home $300 million in just three years, was charged with evading $1 million in sales tax on paintings. The boss of ImClone was accused of insider trading; the founder of Adelphia was charged with defrauding investors. (Nobody was particularly surprised when a survey showed that 82 percent of chief executives admitted to cheating at golf.)[34] Meanwhile, investors fumed when they discovered that Wall Street analysts had been misleading them with Orwellian doublespeak: to the cognoscenti, a 'buy' recommendation meant 'hold' and 'hold' meant 'run like hell.'

What had gone wrong? Two explanations emerged. The first, to which the Bush administration initially subscribed, might be described as the 'bad apples' school: the scandals were the product of individual greed, not a flawed system. The bankruptcies and the arrests would be enough: the founder of Adelphia, John Rigas, was forced to do a 'perp walk,' clamped into handcuffs and paraded in front of the cameras.

By contrast, those of the 'rotten roots' school argued that the problems went much deeper. They argued that the 1990s had seen a dramatic weakening of proper checks and balances. Outside directors had compromised themselves by having questionable financial relationships with the firms that they were supposed to oversee. Too many government regulators had been recruited from the ranks of the industries that they were supposed to police. Above all, auditors had come to see themselves as corporate advisers, not the shareholders' scorekeepers. In short, the agency problem – the question of how to align the interests of those who ran companies with the interest of those who owned them – had returned.

To begin with, it seemed that little would happen. As late as June 2002, Paul Sarbanes, the chairman of the Senate Banking, Housing, and Urban Affairs Committee and a long-standing critic of lax regulation in the boardroom, could not even muster sufficient votes on his own committee to pass a package of auditing reforms, in the face of frantic lobbying by accountants and skepticism from the White House. But as the scandals spread, the politicians realized they had to do something. In mid-July the Senate passed a toughened version of the Sarbanes bill by 97–0, and the president rapidly signed it into law. The law is particularly tough on auditors: the accounting partners who oversee the audit of a specific company have to be rotated every five years, and accounting firms are banned from providing consulting to companies they audit. The law also requires CEOs and chief financial officers to certify the accuracy of their financial reports, and it creates a new crime of securities fraud, making it punishable by up to twenty-five years in jail.

This was indeed a victory for the 'rotten roots' school – probably the most important change in the oversight of American companies since the 1930s. But that claim merits two caveats. First, it was far less revolutionary than the barrage of laws that Roosevelt forced through (which, among other things, created the SEC and separated investment banking from commercial banking). The main contribution of Sarbanes was to tidy up the bit Roosevelt left out – by establishing clear standards and oversight for the accounting industry. Second, plenty of people in the 'rotten roots' school thought that the company needed more tinkering: that a majority of its directors should be independent; that chief executives should be made still more responsible for their firms' performance; that stock options should be formally curtailed; that auditing firms (not just the partners within them) should be rotated.

These shortcomings opened up the possibility that the backlash was only just beginning. Looking back through history, most periods of gaudy capitalism have been followed by a reaction – often an overreaction (the Bubble Act arguably did almost as much harm as the South Sea Bubble). Yet the chances were that the various seers who proclaimed that the American company would never be the same again were whistling in the wind.

To begin with, the 'bad apples' school had been proved right in one respect: the market began to correct itself. Older faces began to appear at the tops of companies; large numbers of companies tried to improve the performance of their boards, not least because their directors were worried that they might be exposed to the sort of problems that had ruined the lives of Enron's directors; many big companies, including Coca-Cola, announced that they would start expensing stock options; accountancy firms became tougher with their clients.

Next, politics was more on the side of the bosses than people realized: the fact that most Americans now owned stocks loaded the dice heavily against full-throated populism. Stock owners have a natural interest in improving the oversight of companies (through better accounting, more independent directorships, better regulation of corporate pensions); they have less interest in imposing constraints on companies' performance.

Most fundamentally, despite the crowing in Europe, the fuss about Enron looked less like a revolution against American capitalism than a restatement of its basic principles. Forcing auditors and outside directors to represent shareholders was not a challenge to the company, but a reaffirmation of it. There was nothing particularly 'corporate' about hiding debts in dodgy partnerships or spending $6,000 on a gold-and-burgundy floral-patterned shower curtain – and then charging it to the company that you ran (as the head of Tyco did). This was not a backlash against business but against bad business practices. Reform should ultimately increase the appeal of shareholder capitalism abroad.

All the same, it is hard to avoid the fact that the American corporation – the trendsetter for the company for most of the previous century – ended the period covered by this book not on a high note, but in a slough of self-doubt, with society peering questioningly at it. An old debate about whether companies were supposed merely to make money legally or to be active instruments for the common good had appeared once again (the difference this time being that while companies as a whole were vastly more powerful, individual companies were vastly more fragile). A full-scale backlash might be avoided, but there was every likelihood of continuing encroachment by government – of more rules, more obligations, more responsibilities. Many of the frustrations and expectations about what the company owed to society focused on one particular sort of company that is the focus of our next chapter: the multinational.

Agents of Influence: Multinationals
     1850–2002

Few companies have attracted as much opprobrium as multinationals. Long before the emergence of modern joint-stock companies, the Medicis and Rothschilds exuded an air of sinister power and fleet-footed mystery. Multinationals have always aroused suspicion – from national elites (who have seen them as threats to their rightful authority), from conservative populists (who have condemned them as agents of cosmopolitanism), and, later, from socialists (who have anathematized them as 'the highest stage of capitalism'). The young Merchant of Prato's hurried flight from Avignon in 1382 would have seemed woefully familiar to Jewish business families in Europe in the 1930s, or more recently to overseas Chinese tycoons in Asia.

There is more to this prejudice than xenophobia. Nation-states like to think of themselves as masters of their own domains; multinationals have loyalties that transcend national boundaries. In poorer parts of the world, the political power, real or imagined, of rich-world companies can seem particularly intrusive. In Asia, Latin America, and Africa, foreign companies built much of the local infrastructure, and uncovered much of the wealth. Yet even when the foreigner's sympathies lay with the country – think of Charles Gould in *Nostromo* – it has been easy for locals to assume otherwise. Even in rich countries, where the threat to the state is nonexistent, multinationals arouse suspicion.

The only reason why a multinational thrives in a foreign

country is that, through fair means or foul, it is better at selling its goods and services than its local competitors. That is seldom a popular proposition.

THE FIRST FORAYS ABROAD

Inevitably, the history of the multinational mirrors that of the company as a whole: it was an idea that started in Europe and first flowered in nineteenth-century Britain, but has since been taken over by the Americans.

The first businesses to coordinate their activities across borders on a large scale were banks. In the Middle Ages, Italian bankers representing the papacy collected part of the English wool crop in Church taxes, transferred it overseas, and took their cut from the transaction. In the sixteenth century, German bankers, such as the Fuggers and the Hochstetters, built up multinational networks whose core business was lending money to cash-hungry rulers – most notably the Holy Roman Emperor and the king of Spain; they then sprawled into other businesses such as mining.

The next conspicuous set of multinationals – the chartered companies such as the East India Company – owed even more to the state (see chapter 2). But the history of the modern multinational – like that of the modern company itself – begins in Britain with the railways.

From the start, the railway was seen as an export industry. Robert Stephenson, the inventor of the Rocket, acted as a surveyor for a railway in Caracas. (The company that employed him had such extensive interests in Latin America that it maintained a newspaper in London called the *American Monitor*.)[1] The early Belgian rail network was almost entirely British-owned, while the first connections from Paris to the French

Channel ports were developed by the London and Southampton Railway Company. Thomas Brassey, one of the greatest mid-Victorian entrepreneurs, constructed almost eight thousand miles of railways in almost every European country. He employed a vast army of eighty thousand engineers and navvies, maintained a locomotive and carriage works in Rouen, and, at one time, was at work on railways and docks in five continents.[2]

In the United States, British companies were largely passive investors. But elsewhere they often built the railways themselves, shipping in British managers, materials, equipment, and labor. Early railway companies often had two boards of directors, one based in London and mainly concerned with financial management, the other in the relevant countries, concerned with day-to-day operations.

The Victorian joint-stock companies copied this model in their other big foray overseas – the search for valuable raw materials. Gold, diamonds, and copper in Africa, tin in Malaya and Bolivia, rubber in Malaya, tea in India, oil in the Middle East: getting hold of these substances entailed establishing multinational companies, with different boards in different places. Hence the mixed ancestry of many of the most famous extractors, such as De Beers (British and South African), Rio Tinto (British and Spanish), and even Shell (British and Dutch).

In the last quarter of the nineteenth century, the multinational changed shape in two ways. First, it broke free from its heavy industrial casing: railways and miners lost their preeminence to companies venturing overseas to sell pharmaceuticals, cigarettes, chocolate, soap, margarine, sewing machines, and ready-made clothes. These were helped by the fact that the world was shrinking faster than ever before, thanks to railroads, steamships, the telegraph and telephone, and, at the end of the period, the automobile. But the second way in which the multinational changed shape was that it had to contort itself to deal with politics – particularly tariffs.

One country after another raised protective tariffs in a bid to stimulate its native industries, starting with America in 1883 and Germany in 1887. By the First World War, Britain and the Netherlands were the only important countries that still flew the free-trade flag. This forced companies that might have preferred to be exporters to become multinationals. William Lever, the British soap king who ended up with factories throughout Europe, Australasia, and America, even claimed that in a free-trading world, there would be no need for him to manufacture soap anywhere but in Britain.[3]

Such barriers affected multinationals of all sorts – but the most exposed were the British, who pioneered the form. In the late nineteenth century, Britain exported capital equivalent to 5 to 10 percent of its GNP. Much of that went into buying foreign stocks, but one historian, John Dunning, has calculated that Britain was responsible for about 45 percent of the $14.3 billion in accumulated foreign direct investment by 1914.[4] It had around two hundred big multinational companies, roughly five times as many as America. And while American (and for that matter German) companies tended to invest in their backyards, Britain took the whole world as its playpen.

The simplest sort of British multinational was a successful domestic firm that ventured abroad in search of markets and supplies. Roughly half of Britain's thirty largest companies had at least one factory abroad by 1914, with consumer-goods firms, such as Lever and J&P Coats, leading the pack.[5] Unlike the Americans, who tended to venture abroad only when they reached a critical size at home, some relatively small British firms went international. The Gramophone Company (which eventually became EMI) had factories in India, Russia, France,

Spain, and Austria by 1914. Albright & Wilson, a small phosphorus company in the West Midlands with a staff of a few hundred, had factories in both Canada and the United States in the same year. In the chocolate business, Mackintosh, a small firm, established factories in the United States and Germany, while the market leaders, Cadbury, Fry, and Rowntree, contented themselves with exporting.[6]

However, Britain had another set of multinational companies that were specifically founded on overseas trade. The most numerous sort, the so-called 'free-standing companies,' were normally headquartered in London, but specifically created to do business in another country.[7] These companies gloried in names like the Anglo-Argentine, the Anglo-Australian, and the Anglo-Russian. Each of them was highly specialized, but together they covered the entire gamut of business, from meatpacking in Argentina to mortgages in Australia. In a slightly different bracket, there was also a group of overseas traders, led by Swire and Jardine Matheson, that were established by Britons in the colonies, in order to facilitate trade around the region. The traders soon developed factories of their own. In 1895, for instance, Jardine established the Ewo Cotton Spinning and Weaving Company in Shanghai.

Yet, for all their pioneering spirit, the British were hobbled abroad by the same thing that hobbled them at home – unprofessional management. It was considered ungentlemanly for parent companies to exercise too much control over their foreign subsidiaries. Before the First World War, the foreign branches of firms like Dunlop, Courtaulds, and Vickers reported their affairs when and where they wanted.[8] The head offices of most British multinationals were not famed for their dynamism: witness *Psmith in the City*, P. G Wodehouse's 1910 novel about a young Etonian trying to avoid hard work at the

New Asiatic Bank, based on the author's own brief stint at the Hong Kong & Shanghai Banking Corporation.

The Germans were more systematic, if less adventurous. Germany also had plenty of overseas trading companies – or mercantile houses, as they were known. Yet, the typical German multinational was a successful domestic company that expanded abroad in search of markets and raw materials – first to Austria-Hungary and soon afterward to the United States, where German immigrants provided both willing customers and a ready-made network of contacts.

Germany was much more successful than Britain in producing high-tech multinationals, particularly in the chemical and electrical sectors. It also began to develop international consumer brands. A. W. Faber, the famous pencil company, expanded overseas as early as the 1870s, with branches in Paris and London, an agency in Vienna, and a factory in Brooklyn, New York.[9] And where German manufacturers went, so did their banks, working much like the British trading houses, opening up markets, such as oil in the Middle East, for their customers.

Most other European countries spawned multinationals. France was the second-largest capital exporter in Europe after Britain. The St. Gobain glassworks had already built a branch plant in Germany by 1850: by 1914, it was also manufacturing in Italy, Belgium, Holland, Spain, and Austria-Hungary. Société Schneider et Cie owned utility companies in Morocco, invested in collieries in Belgium, and helped to develop the Russian armaments industry.[10] Société Générale de Belgique made direct investments in Latin America, China, and the Congo, as well as a clutch of European countries. The Swiss probably invested more abroad than at home. By 1900, Nestlé had built factories in America, France, Norway, Austria, and Great

Britain.[11] Even Europe's weaker economies succeeded in producing a few multinationals. Fiat expanded from its Turin base with factories in Austria, the United States, and Russia by 1913. By the same year, the First Bulgarian Insurance Company of Roustchouk operated in nine countries.

Meanwhile, Asian companies also began to expand overseas. By 1914, Japan was investing about a tenth of its GNP abroad – a good deal of it in the form of direct investment in China (particularly Manchuria).[12] Trading companies such as Mitsui opened branches in China from the late 1870s onward. In 1902, Mitsui started a fashion for building cotton plants in China. Ten years later, the Japanese owned 886 power looms in China, even more than the British.[13] The Japanese also tiptoed into the United States. As early as 1881, fourteen Japanese trading companies had branches in New York.[14] Three trading companies later opened offices in Texas to handle their cotton business.[15] In 1892, Kikkoman built a factory in Denver, Colorado, to make soy sauce for Japanese immigrants.[16]

Many nineteenth-century multinationals – particularly the European ones – were bound up with imperialism, though never quite to the extent of the East India Company. The most ghastly abuses occurred in the Congo Free State, the private empire set up in the 1880s by King Leopold of Belgium. Strapped for cash, the king sold off parts of the country to various *concessionaire* companies, in which he often kept half the shares himself. In the 1890s, when demand for rubber surged, the *concessionaire* companies assembled their workforce through torture. The profits were so large that the French imitated the *concessionaire* system in their part of the Congo in 1900. But public outcry, prompted by the publication of a damning report by the British consul, Roger Casement, mounted, and in 1908, the Belgian government was forced to annex the Congo Free State, paying off Leopold.

More often, though, multinationals were not so much imperialist despoilers as imperialist builders – of institutions, of infrastructure, and of confidence. In Africa and Latin America, mining companies found themselves obliged to invest in railways and schools. The princely hongs of Jardine and Swire did as much to create Hong Kong as the British government. Many colonial officers retired to join British companies, taking their Kiplingesque ideas about imperial duty with them.

Yet, the link between the nineteenth-century multinationals and imperialism has often been exaggerated, particularly by devotees of the Marxist idea that imperialism was the highest stage of capitalism. Most foreign direct investment in the period flowed to other developed countries rather than to the colonies. The impoverished tribesmen of Africa hardly provided much demand for Western products. For the most part, the logic of nineteenth-century imperialism was strategic rather than commercial. The competitive landgrabs by European countries in Africa brought few commercial gains. Some businessmen may have made money in these distant colonies; most did not. The embittered rubber planters of Somerset Maugham's short stories were more typical of the breed than Cecil Rhodes or the Oppenheimers.

AN EMPIRE OF THEIR OWN

One indirect sign of this is that the strongest challenge to Britain's lead came not from its fellow European imperialists but from American business. By 1914, a growing number of American companies had factories abroad, including such familiar names as Ford, Eastman Kodak, Quaker Oats, and Coca-Cola. Direct foreign investment amounted to about 7 percent of America's gross national product.[17] By 1950, at the latest, America had firmly replaced Britain as the world's premier progenitor of multinationals.

The most important reason for the rise of the Americans is the one that we have discussed in chapter 4. The same skills that allowed American firms to command a continent-sized market at home also enabled them to sell their products around the world. They were the first to learn how to exploit an economy in which labor was relatively scarce and workers were reasonably well paid, the first to master mass production and mass marketing.

Industrial companies were the first Americans to make their mark abroad. In 1867, the Singer Sewing Machine Company opened a plant in Britain. In 1884, Thomson-Houston, one of the many firms that were later absorbed into General Electric, established an international division. Ford built a plant at Trafford Park in Manchester in 1908, assembling its cars from imported components; a mere five years later, Ford was Britain's largest car producer. In 1914, two of the largest businesses in Russia were Singer and International Harvester. Singer had a workforce of 27,000 and a sales force whose travels took them to outermost Siberia.[18]

This makes the Americans seem remorseless. In fact, many of them acquired their overseas operations in the same way the British acquired their empire – 'in a fit of absence of mind.' American firms established makeshift foreign marketing departments to cope with spontaneous demand for their products. But once they had entered foreign markets, they found themselves sucked in farther, often, ironically, by protectionists trying to keep out imports. In 1897, for example, Count Goluchowski, the Austrian foreign minister, distributed a circular letter to other European leaders urging them to band together against the American invaders. By establishing affiliates in Europe, American firms could leap over tariffs, get their goods to market faster, and adapt them to local taste. Inevitably, there was a snowball effect: no sooner had a company like Ford moved abroad than its competitors and suppliers felt compelled to do likewise.

After the First World War, the Americans became more methodical. Even Britain, the last free-trading nation, introduced tariffs on some goods, including cars, in 1916, before fully surrendering to protectionism in 1932. Yet none of the tariff barriers were proof against Yankee ingenuity. In the 1920s, General Motors bought Britain's Vauxhall car company and Germany's Opel to get around the new tariffs. 'We had to devise some methods of living with restrictive regulations and duties,' recalled Alfred Sloan. 'We had to work out a special form of organization that would be suitable overseas.' (In some cases, this desire 'to go local' led to an unhealthy cohabitation with tyrants: witness the way that IBM and Ford cozied up to Hitler.) Meanwhile, the Americans also began to spread their wings beyond the safety of Canada and Western Europe. In the Depression-racked 1930s, a miserable time for multinationals of all sorts, the Americans found their fastest growth in Latin America.

By 1938, the total stock of foreign direct investment had grown, by Dunning's estimates, to $26.4 billion, of which 40 percent was British and 28 percent was American. The postwar years saw the United States decisively seize Britain's lead. The Second World War might almost have been designed to give American multinationals the final edge over their European competitors. After the war, rising European living standards, courtesy of the Marshall Plan, stimulated consumer demand, which America's healthier companies were best placed to satisfy. The introduction of the General Agreement on Tariffs and Trade (GATT) in 1947 swept away most of the previous tariff barriers, and American firms pushed overseas rapidly. By 1960, the global stock of accumulated foreign direct investment had swollen to $66 billion – and the United States held 49 percent of this, compared with Britain's 16 percent.[19]

One of America's secret weapons was the passenger jet. The itinerant international manager was not new. Expatriate managers from Shell and Unilever were to be found the world over, but their job was to put down local roots rather than flit hither and thither. The new breed of American multinational men spent their lives traveling on jets between one anonymous hotel room and another. They could jet across the Atlantic (or the 'pond' as the more irritating among them called it) in seven hours. They could stay in touch with their offices back home by phone and telex. The obvious downside of this was superficiality, but it also allowed the Americans to look upon their companies as global entities rather than as a collection of national companies.

The 1960s were the heyday of the American multinational. Europeans watched in horror as American direct investment in the Continent grew from $1.7 billion in 1950 to $24.5 billion in 1970, and an army of American invaders – IBM, Ford, Kellogg, Heinz, Procter & Gamble – marched across their continent. In *The American Challenge* (1967), Jean-Jacques Servan-Schreiber argued that America's superior ability to manage big companies over wide geographical areas was making it impossi-ble for European companies to compete. The Americans, he pointed out, had mastered the tools of organization that held the key to prosperity; the Europeans, on the other hand, were held back by their commitment to family firms and their cult of flair rather than science.

For critics everywhere, the evil of the new breed was symbolized by ITT. Born as a tiny telephone business in Puerto Rico in 1920, the conglomerate first distinguished itself by sucking up to assorted dictators, including Franco in Spain and Hitler in Germany. (ITT's German subsidiaries had a hand in making Hitler's Focke-Wulf bombers, and after the war the company successfully claimed compensation for the destruction of the Focke-Wulf plants by Allied bombers.)[20] In the postwar period, it sprawled across the world, bribing and cajoling local politicians as it went. In the 1970s, the company intervened in Chile in an attempt to stop Allende's left-wing government coming to power. The Securities and Exchange Commission eventually revealed that ITT had spent a total of $8.7 million in illegal activities in countries such as Indonesia, Iran, the Philippines, Algeria, Mexico, Italy, and Turkey.

THE MULTICULTURAL MULTINATIONAL

In fact, the idea that the Americans would sweep all before them collapsed in the 1970s. The devaluation of the dollar in 1971 made foreign assets look more costly to American firms and American ones cheaper to foreigners. The oil-price hikes in the middle of the decade and the subsequent rise in commodity prices boosted the demand for energy-saving devices that Americans had little experience in producing. Inflation and recession further dented their self-confidence. By the early 1980s, the Americans were on the defensive, pinned back by German multinationals and humiliated by the Japanese (see chapter 7).

Trying to view the history of multinationals through nationalistic lenses becomes harder in the final quarter of the twentieth century. This, after all, was a time when the business sections of bookshops groaned with titles such as *The Border-*

less World, The Twilight of Sovereignty, and *Sovereignty at Bay.*
A famous essay in the *Harvard Business Review* in 1983 by
Theodore Levitt argued that 'the earth is round but for most
purposes, it is sensible to treat it as flat.' That was overstating it.
Geography did still matter. In 1995, the top one hundred companies by market valuation included forty-three from the United
States, twenty-seven from Japan, eleven from Great Britain, and
five from Germany. Countries as big as Russia, China, India,
Canada, Indonesia, and Brazil could not claim any.[21] Yet, this
was the period when multinationals could appear from anywhere. Two of the world's most successful mobile-telephone
companies, Nokia and Ericksson, sprang up on the edge of the
Arctic Circle. Acer, the third largest computer company in the
world by 2000, was founded in Taiwan, a place that was once
synonymous with cheap radios.[22]

This period saw three important changes that affected multinationals of all sorts. The first was a huge increase in their
numbers. By 2001, there were about sixty-five thousand
'transnational' companies in the world, roughly five times the
number in 1975; around the globe they gathered together
850,000 foreign affiliates, employed 54 million people, and had
revenues of $19 trillion. In the 1990s, foreign direct investment
grew four times faster than world output and three times faster
than world trade. Roughly a third of trade flows consisted of
payments within individual companies, reflecting the way that
multinational production systems stretched around the world.
In 2000, the total global figure for FDI passed $1 trillion.

Second, smaller companies did as much to drive globalization in this period as bigger ones. The lowering of trade barriers,
the spread of deregulation, the plummeting cost of transport
and communication: all made it possible for Davids to challenge Goliaths. Freer trade made it possible for young

companies, including Microsoft, to reach overseas markets, without having to build huge foreign offices. The deregulation of the capital markets allowed smaller companies to borrow serious money, while innovative management techniques, such as just-in-time production, allowed them to mimic the efficiencies of bigger competitors. Small companies also encountered fewer political prejudices than big ones.[23]

Third, multinationals tried harder to treat the world as a single market, embracing ugly names like 'transnationals,' 'metanationals,' and 'new age multinationals.' The change was particularly marked in big companies. For most of the twentieth century, Ford was essentially a confederation of national companies. Each country had its own head offices, design facilities, and production plants. At one point, Ford even had two Escort cars on the road that had been designed and built entirely separately. Yet, by the 1990s, it was developing 'world cars' with common parts, like the aptly named Mondeo, coordinating not just its manufacturing but its advertising on a global scale.

This all sounds rather imperial. In fact, good multinationals went to great lengths not just to adapt products to local taste (even dividing up the American market), but also to scour the world for ideas. Indeed, in an age where most markets could be accessed easily, the only justification for having people on the ground everywhere was to use their brains.[24] Multinationals spent fortunes on new electronic systems to speed messages around their organizations, and they began to experiment with what might be called intellectual arbitrage – putting Italian designers together with Japanese specialists in miniaturization, for example.

Many of the organizational changes of these years were driven by the desire to combine global scale with local knowledge. Nestlé put the headquarters of its pasta business in Italy.

At Asea Brown Boveri, a Swedish-Swiss merger set up in 1988, Percy Barnevik decentralized some things (dividing the firm into thirteen hundred separate companies that were also subdivided into five thousand profit centers) and centralized others: he made English his firm's official language, although only a third of the employees spoke it as their mother tongue, and appointed a Praetorian guard of international managers to oversee the firm.

Yet this did not provide a definitive answer. ABB went into rapid decline in 2002, as its matrices got hopelessly complicated. A bigger problem was that too many multinationals still assumed that 'global' simply meant 'more international.' Most drew their leaders overwhelmingly from their home countries. Even such paragons of multiculturalism as Unilever and Shell could produce precious few senior officers from China and Brazil, two of the most promising markets of the twenty-first century. And some firms looked on the developing world as a source of cheap labor rather than ideas. This 'Nike economy,' relying on cheap Third World workers, helped stir up a backlash against multinationals.

THE GREAT UNLOVED

By the end of the twentieth century, multinationals were routinely denounced as the dark lords of globalization. Antiglobalization protesters rioted in Seattle, Washington, and London to protest against the awesome power of multinationals, raging against companies like McDonald's, which by the mid-1990s was serving 3 million burgers a day in one hundred countries. Raymond Vernon, the author of one of the classic studies of multinationals, *Sovereignty at Bay*, used his last book, *In the Hurricane's Eye* (1998), to predict a gloomy future for multinationals, as people turned against them.

Had they really become so powerful? Businesspeople were partly to blame for the notion. They had long dreamed, as the chairman of Dow Chemical once put it, 'of buying an island owned by no nation and of establishing the world headquarters of the Dow company on the truly neutral ground of such an island, beholden to no nation or society.' It suited corporate chieftains to give the impression that their companies could raise camp and desert any government that disappointed them.

In fact, multinationals were considerably less powerful than their critics imagined. The idea, popular in antiglobalization circles, that companies accounted for fifty-one of the world's one hundred biggest economies relied on comparing the sales of companies with the GDP of countries. But GDP is a measure of value added, not sales. Using a measure for value added for companies, only thirty-seven multinationals appeared in the one hundred biggest economies in the world in 2000; and only two of them scraped into the top fifty (Wal-Mart in forty-fourth place, and Exxon in forty-eighth). Wal-Mart was barely a quarter of the size of a fairly small European country, such as Belgium and Austria, though it was bigger than Pakistan and Peru. Far from gaining economic clout, the biggest multinationals were losing it. In the period 1980 to 2000, the world's biggest fifty firms grew more slowly than the world economy as a whole.[25]

Besides, wealth is not the same as power. In 2000, Wal-Mart might have been richer than Peru, but set beside the government of even that dysfunctional country, it looked pretty feeble. Wal-Mart had no powers of coercion: it could not tax, raise armies, or imprison people. In each of the countries where it operated, it had to bow down to local governments. Previous giants such as ITT or the East India Company could muster real political power; Wal-Mart was simply rather good at retailing.

The history of multinationals points to two contradictory conclusions. The first is that multinationals have generally become a force for good – or, at the very least, that they have given up sinning quite so egregiously. The early chartered companies were state monopolies, with a penchant for conquest and exploitation. The initials of the Royal African Company were branded on the chests of thousands of slaves – and the RAC was warmly backed not just by the state (its first president was James, Duke of York, after whom New York was named), but also by civil society (its shareholders included John Locke, that great philosopher of liberty). 'In the East, the laws of society, the laws of nature have been enormously violated,' argued the Burgoyne Committee in 1773 in its damnation of the East India Company. 'Oppression in every shape has ground the faces of the poor defenseless natives; and tyranny in her bloodless form has stalked abroad.'[26]

This tradition of exploitation certainly continued into the nineteenth century. The report by the British consul, Roger Casement, on the administration of the Congo Free State makes horrifying reading. A sentry who worked for one of the *concessionaire* companies explained how he was holding eleven women hostage until their husbands 'brought in the right amount of rubber required of them on the next market day.'[27] Yet, by the late twentieth century, the sins of the multinationals, with a few exceptions, such as ITT, tended to be less of commission than of omission: for instance, Shell was roundly criticized for not doing more to prevent the execution of Ken Sarowiwa, a Nigerian dissident, in 1995. They did not go around overthrowing governments.

What about the objection that multinationals paid abysmal wages? Here the vital question is whether the wages were 'abysmal' by Western or local standards. In 1994, the average wage at the foreign affiliates of multinationals was one and a half times the local average; in the case of low-income countries the figure was double the local domestic manufacturing wage.[28] Multinationals have usually abided by higher labor standards than their local rivals. The key to their success is not usually that they pay low wages. It is that they bring superior capital, skills, and ideas (which push up living standards and increase the choices open to local consumers).

The provision of better goods and services – everything from washing machines to checking accounts and even hamburgers – has always been the central justification of multinational business. It stands by itself. Yet, it is also worth recording that multinationals have not always been motivated solely by greed. Around the world, they have built schools and hospitals. Even the more sordid episodes in their history usually stand beside examples of decency. In 1910, William Lever traveled to the wretched Belgian Congo and took over a vast area of about seven enormous plantations, where he started to build a more rudimentary version of Port Sunlight. His model community included hospitals, schools, and roads. The Congo did not turn a single penny of profit in his lifetime, but Lever regarded these villages as one of his greatest achievements.[29]

The second conclusion is that multinationals have never been loved, either at home or abroad. We have already mentioned the xenophobia of Trollope and the Morning Post. In 1902, a British commentator, F. A. Mackenzie, published The American Invaders – a no-holds-barred denunciation of the American multinationals that were planting factories on British soil. For much of the twentieth century, the British Left fumed about foreign investment on the grounds that it was robbing an English workman somewhere of his livelihood, an argument that J. A. Hobson (and later Lenin) worked up into an entire theory of imperialism. Years later, Pat Buchanan and Ross Perot were singing from the same hymnbook.

It would be easy to pass these off as examples of economic illiteracy, political opportunism, and xenophobia. But multinationals clearly arouse fears that are too deep-rooted to be dug up with a few statistics. There is something worrying about the idea that your job is dependent on the decisions of managers who live in faraway places. Thus, multinationals will continue to represent much of what is best about companies: their capacity to improve productivity and therefore the living standards of ordinary people. But they will also continue to embody what is most worrying – perhaps most alienating – about companies as well.

Conclusion: The Future of the Company

In 1912, Woodrow Wilson, then on the verge of becoming president, surveyed American society with evident dismay. He lamented the rise of vast corporations, and the way that they were transforming freeborn Americans into mere cogs in the great industrial machine. 'We are in the presence of a new organization of society,' he wrote. 'Our life has broken away from the past.'[1]

The company has been deeply involved in most of the great 'breaks with the past' since at least the middle of the nineteenth century. Even when it has not directed them itself, it has shown, to borrow a phrase from Henry Adams, a remarkable ability to 'condense' social changes. That condensing has not just been a matter of churning out society-changing products, like the Model T or Microsoft Word, but of changing the way that people behave – by disrupting old social orders, by dictating the pace of daily life.

Throughout its history, the company has shown an equally remarkable ability to evolve: indeed, that has been the secret of its success. In the nineteenth century, the company transformed itself from an instrument of government to a 'little republic' of its own, charged with running its own affairs and making its shareholders money. In the twentieth century, Wilson's 'new organization' outlived the robber barons whom he so feared, and allied itself instead with their hired servants. Company Man turned the organization into a smooth-running bureaucratic machine, but when conditions changed, he, too, was jettisoned; now the company presents itself to the world as a lean, flattened entrepreneurial creation.

There can be little doubt that such an amoebic creature will continue to change shape dramatically in the coming years – and that those changes will bring with them 'breaks with the past' for all of us. Where will these changes take us? That depends on two things that have been themes throughout this book. The first is economic logic: the balance between transaction costs and hierarchy costs that decides whether companies make sense. The second is political. Companies sprang from the loins of the state. Even when they were set free in the mid-nineteenth century, they still had to secure what might be called 'a franchise from society.'[2] The terms of that franchise may be explicit or implicit, but when companies have appeared to break them, society in the shape of people like Woodrow Wilson has reined in companies, often crudely. 'I believe in corporations,' proclaimed Wilson's contemporary and rival, Teddy Roosevelt. 'They are indispensable instruments of our modern civilization; but I believe that they should be so supervised and so regulated that they shall act for the interests of the community as a whole.' The same was said (albeit less eloquently) by virtually all the American politicians debating the Sarbanes-Oxley bill in 2002.

THREE POSSIBLE WORLDS

From the purely economic standpoint, three different futures for the company present themselves. The first – particularly popular in antiglobalization circles – holds that a handful of giant companies are engaged in a 'silent takeover' of the world. The past couple of decades have seen an unprecedented spurt of mergers.

The survivors, it is maintained, are the real lords of the universe today – with more economic power than most nation-states, but without any sense of responsibility or accountability.

The trouble with this view is that few facts support it. As we have seen, the idea that most of the one hundred biggest economies of the world are now companies is a gross abuse of statistics. Rather than increasing their hold over the universe, big companies have been losing ground. National markets that only thirty years ago seemed comfortable oligopolies – such as America's television and car markets – are now squabbled over by companies from the world over. And, in general, the more futuristic the industry, the less the evidence of concentration. In computer hardware, computer software, and long-distance telephony, the market share of the top five firms in America has been declining.[3]

The second school of thought argues almost the opposite of the first: that companies are becoming ever less substantial. For a glimpse of the future, its proponents recommend the Monorail Corporation, which sells computers. Monorail owns no factories, warehouses, or any other tangible asset. It operates from a single floor that it leases in an office building in Atlanta. Its computers are designed by freelance workers. To place orders, customers call a toll-free number connected to Federal Express's logistics service, which passes the orders on to a contract manufacturer that assembles the computers from various parts. FedEx then ships the computers to the customers and sends the invoices to the SunTrust Bank, Monorail's agent. The company is not much of anything except a good idea, a handful of people in Atlanta, and a bunch of contracts.[4]

This minimalist school has the benefit, by and large, of having some distinguished economists on its side. If you use Ronald Coase's premise that companies make sense when the 'transaction costs' associated with buying things on the market exceed the hierarchical costs of maintaining a bureaucracy, then modern technology is generally shifting the balance of advantage away from companies and toward markets and individuals. Yet, the idea that the company will retreat to the periphery of the economy looks farfetched. Big companies, as we have seen, possess certain 'core competences,' usually cultural ones, that cannot easily be purchased on the market. And even leaving culture aside, there are still market failures that persuade firms to try to do things internally rather than externally (companies will always be tempted to buy suppliers that provide goods that they cannot get elsewhere). Microsoft and Oracle may be far looser, more fragile organizations than Sloan's General Motors, but they are still large companies, trying to get bigger.

The third forecast is an offshoot of the second: that the discrete company is no longer the basic building block of the modern economy. It will be replaced by the 'network.' Some economies have long centered on webs of interlocking businesses, such as Japan's *keiretsu* and South Korea's *chaebol*. But the models most commonly cited are the boundaryless firms of Silicon Valley. In theory, these loose-fitting alliances are the ideal homes for Peter Drucker's knowledge workers.

This sounds attractive. But the networking concept has (appropriately enough) bundled together too many contradictory ideas. The older sort of networks, like the *keiretsu*, which were largely attempts to shield member companies from the market, are now being pulled apart by it. The networks in Silicon Valley, which rely on their sensitivity to market movements, look far more modern, but they are still built around companies. Whatever its other faults, the joint-stock company possesses both a legal personality and a system of internal accountability; networks have neither. This makes it difficult for them to make joint decisions or to divide up profits (witness the desperate attempts of Airbus to become a stand-alone company). Where a network succeeds, it is usually because a firm is driving it. Without that, a tendency to agonize over the most mundane decisions takes over.[5]

So none of these three futures looks inevitable. Yet, the last two visions seem more plausible than the first. The trend at the moment is for the corporation to become ever less 'corporate': for bigger organizations to break themselves down into smaller entrepreneurial units. The erosion of Coasean transaction costs will make it ever easier for small companies – or just collections of entrepreneurs – to challenge the dominance of big companies; and ever more tempting for entrepreneurs to enter into loose relationships with other entrepreneurs rather than to form long-lasting corporations.

A FRANCHISE UNDER THREAT

The trouble with all these economic forecasts is that they ignore a decisive variable: politics. A persistent theme of this book has been the jostling for power between the company and government. The balance has unquestionably swung in the company's favor. The modern firm is not in the same position as the East India Company, which had to go cap in hand to parliament every twenty years to renew its charter. Companies have often profited from 'races to the bottom' by forcing governments and American states to compete for their favors. They have also encroached on the prerogatives of nation-states and embedded themselves in the body politic: think of the effect of corporate advertising or modern corporate control of the media. Companies have sometimes been able to outfight even the most powerful governments: IBM survived the American government's biggest antitrust case of the 1970s; Microsoft seems to have thwarted the biggest assault of the 1990s.

So the balance may have shifted, but it is far from clear that the company is now the stronger force. As we have already pointed out in our comparison of Wal-Mart and Peru, even the biggest company has few real powers to match those of a state, no matter how shambolic the latter is. Companies are also more heavily regulated and policed than ever: they may not have to justify their existence every twenty years to parliament, but they have to deal with outside inspection, from both government and the media, on a far more frequent basis than the East India Company ever did. As for races to the bottom, these are surely limited by the fact that many companies owe their success to geographical location. Companies cannot uproot themselves on a whim, because doing so means leaving behind the staff and customers they need to thrive. Microsoft never threatened to quit Seattle during its feud with the Justice Department.

To keep on doing business, the modern company still needs a franchise from society, and the terms of that franchise still matter enormously. From the company's point of view, two clouds have gathered on the horizon: the cloud of corporate scandals and the cloud of social responsibility.

We have already described the Enron scandal (see chap-ter 7). Looking forward, it is worth stressing that roguery is, has been, and always will be a problem for companies, particularly during stock-market booms. It is easy to imagine the directors of Enron sitting around a table in Houston, with one eye on their share options, concluding that their real work was 'the privilege of manufacturing shares.' In fact, that phrase comes from a Victorian novel, Trollope's *The Way We Live Now* (1875), which was itself probably based on a real-life scam by a share-hawking finance company called Crédit Mobilier, which, like the villainous Augustus Melmotte, hailed from France. An even closer parallel to Enron is the career of Samuel Insull (1859–1938), who rose from poverty to become one of the most admired businessmen of the roaring 1920s, making Chicago Edison into the base of a gigantic pyramid of utility and transportation companies. At one point, he held sixty-five chairmanships, eighty-five directorships, and eleven presidencies. But the 1929 crash brought this pyramid tumbling down around his ears. Insull fled the country, roundly denounced as a symbol of corporate greed. He was hauled back to the United States for trial and, surprisingly, acquitted, but his fortune had gone, and he died in 1938 on the Paris subway.

Would the world be a better place if the Victorians had listened to the alarmists who suggested banning joint-stock companies after the bankruptcies of the 1860s? Would America be a richer country if the New Dealers had nationalized great chunks of corporate America? Surely not. History suggests caution in the aftermath of Enron. Most of the reforms in the Sarbanes-Oxley Act, such as stopping auditors from doubling as consultants, will surely only enhance the joint-stock company. Other fiddles are still needed: it would have been better if the Sarbanes-Oxley Act had forced a company to rotate its audit firms, not just the partners inside the firm. But the basic rules of capitalism do not need to be rewritten.

This ties into the second element that will determine the company's franchise. Since the mid-nineteenth century, there has been a battle between two different conceptions of the company: the stakeholder ideal that holds that companies are responsible to a wide range of social groups and the shareholder ideal that holds that they are primarily responsible to their shareholders. That debate looks set to intensify, not just because of Enron, but also because the stakeholder ideal is in gradual retreat in its strongholds of Japan and continental Europe. Germany, the spiritual home of stakeholderism, has introduced more IPOs in the past five years than in the previous fifty, and there are now more German shareholders than there are trade unionists. German giants such as DaimlerChrysler and Vodafone Mannesmann are under fire for trying to break 'jobs for life' agreements. The same is happening in Japan and much of the former Communist world. In China, privatized companies are trying to shed social obligations, such as running hospitals, that the state forced on them.

The likelihood is that the Anglo-Saxon model will continue to gain ground, if only because it is more flexible. But is the shareholder model really as heartless and socially irresponsible as its critics claim? You don't have to be a hard-core opponent of globalization to worry about corporate heartlessness. There is a widespread feeling that companies have not fulfilled their part of the social contract: people have been sacked or fear that they are about to be sacked; they work longer hours, see less of their families – all for institutions that Edward Coke castigated four hundred years ago for having no souls.

The broad answer is that although Anglo-Saxon companies may not have souls, they do have brains. Companies now operate in a blaze of publicity; they are more answerable than ever before to their shareholders. By any reasonable measure, they pillage the Third World less than they used to, and they offer more opportunities to women and minorities.

But their defense should not just be based on renouncing bad habits. From the first, Anglo-Saxon companies have generally been willing to take on social obligations without the prompting of governments. The souls of their founders may have had something to do with this. Max Weber famously pointed to the connection between the rise of capitalism and the Protestant ethic. The Quaker businesspeople who founded so many of Britain's banks and confectionery firms had regular meetings in which they justified their business affairs to their peers.[6] The robber barons built much of America's educational and health infrastructure. Companies have become increasingly explicit about their social goals. Silicon Valley's oldest company, Hewlett-Packard, has been arguing that profit is not the main point of its business for more than half a century – and insisting that the HP way is the core of its commercial success. IBM now describes itself as a strategic investor in education, Merck has plowed millions into AIDS eradication, Avon is one of the world's biggest investors in breast cancer research.

Many critics of companies will identify selfish reasons for doing all of this: cosmetics companies want to be seen as sympathetic to women, just as Philadelphia's robber barons wanted to use charity to worm their way into the Whitemarsh Valley Hunt Club. The cynics miss the point. Throughout history, as long as they are making money, companies have repeatedly pursued aims other than simply maximizing their short-term profits. There are plenty of hard-nosed reasons why the corporate sector has a vested interest in being seen to do good.

Consider two reasons that are increasing in importance. The first is trust. Trust gives companies the benefit of the doubt when dealing with customers, workers, and even regulators. The value of acting in a responsible way during a crisis – such as Johnson & Johnson's reaction to cyanide poisoning in Tylenol in 1982 (the drug firm, at great expense, withdrew the product immediately) – has now been drummed into capitalists. By contrast, companies that treat their environments badly forfeit trust. General Electric has lost far more money in terms of publicity and goodwill through polluting the Hudson River than it ever saved by letting waste into the river in the first place. The second reason is the 'war for talent.' Southwest Airlines is one of the most considerate employers in its business: it was the only American airline not to lay people off after September 11. In 2001, the company received 120,000 applications for 3,000 jobs. The decaffeinated 'niceness' of Starbucks has also been a competitive advantage: its employee turnover rate of 50 percent compares with an average of about 250 percent in the fast-food industry.

These achievements are real, but drawing up long lists of when companies have acted responsibly (and when they have not) risks missing the biggest point. Henry Ford's $5 wage was a force for good; but his cheap cars helped change the lives of the poor in ways that socialists could only dream about. Boeing has spent millions of dollars financing good works in Seattle, but the real boost to the region has been the jobs that it has provided. Johnson & Johnson's behavior with Tylenol was exemplary – but its main contribution to American well-being has been all the pills and profits that it has made. The central good of the joint-stock company is that it is the key to productivity growth in the private sector: the best and easiest structure for individuals to pool capital, to refine skills, and to pass them on. We are all richer as a result.

The problems in the future may stem less from what companies do to society than from what society does to companies. Governments may have deregulated markets, but they are regulating companies more enthusiastically than ever. Company oversight that began as a mixture of accident prevention (workplace safety rules) and administrative convenience (organizing pensions through companies) has sprawled. In America, the cumulative effect of laws on everything from disabled people to greenhouse gas amounts to a domestic version of the European Union's Social Chapter, which formally codifies workers' rights. Multinationals are now seen as tools, via fair-trade regulations, for sorting out the evils of Third World poverty. The numbers and the obligations are likely to get larger as politicians discover that it is far cheaper (both in financial and electoral terms) to get companies to do their work for them.

For the burgeoning corporate responsibility movement, this has been all well and good. And, in one way, they have history on their side: for better or worse, the fate of Robert Lowe's 'Little Republics' has always been wound up with the state that originally set them free. But the other lesson from history is that both government and companies have generally prospered most when the line between them has been fairly thick. The foremost contribution of the company to society has been through economic progress. It has an obligation to obey the law. But it is designed to make money.

This debate has continued under different guises for centuries. The twist to the current version is that, while the company in general has never seemed more vibrant, individual companies have never seemed more fragile and insubstantial. The East India Company lasted for 258 years; it would be remarkable if Microsoft reached a quarter of that life span. In a world of limitless choice, no company can rely on a secure future.

Will society find a successful way of exploiting an organization that has become collectively indispensable, yet individually unpredictable? That question should be at the heart of the debate about the future of the corporation. In the meantime, the joint-stock company has plenty to be proud of. The organization that Gilbert and Sullivan celebrated in *Utopia Limited* deserves at least a round of applause for what it has achieved so far.

Bibliographic Note

The indispensable authority on the history of the company is Alfred Chandler. Chandler has produced three classic books: *Strategy and Structure: Chapters in the History of the American Industrial Enterprise* (Cambridge, Mass.: MIT Press, 1962); *The Visible Hand: The Managerial Revolution in American Business* (Cambridge, Mass.: Harvard University Press, 1977); and *Scale and Scope: The Dynamics of Industrial Capitalism* (Cambridge, Mass.: Harvard University Press, 1990). The first two of these books focus on America; the third broadens the argument to include Britain and Germany.

Another great authority is Peter Drucker. His best book on the company is a snapshot of General Motors after the Second World War, *The Concept of the Corporation* (New York: Mentor, 1983; first published in 1946), but historical insights are scattered around his voluminous writings on management.

General books on the history of the company are rare: most historians sensibly prefer to limit themselves by company and period. A handful of books are indispensable. Nathan Rosenberg and L. E. Birdzell's *How the West Grew Rich: The Economic Transformation of the Industrial World* (New York: Basic Books, 1986) is full of insights into the role that companies played in the West's successes. Jonathan Barron Baskin and Paul Miranti's *A History of Corporate Finance* (Cambridge: Cambridge University Press, 1997) is a comprehensive guide to the subject, complete with extensive footnotes. Anthony

Sampson's *Company Man: The Rise and Fall of Corporate Life* (New York: Times Business, 1995) tells the history of the company through the experience of its most loyal servants. *Creating Modern Capitalism: How Entrepreneurs, Companies and Countries Triumphed in Three Industrial Revolutions* (Cambridge, Mass.: Harvard University Press, 1995), edited by Thomas McCraw, contains essays on Britain, Germany, and the United States. *Colossus: How the Corporation Changed America* (New York: Broadway Books, 2001), edited by Jack Beatty, is a useful collection of readings. Another useful collection of essays is *The Political Economy of the Company* (Oxford: Hart, 2000), edited by John Parkinson, Andrew Gamble, and Gavin Kelly. Daniel Yergin and Joseph Stanislaw's *The Commanding Heights: The Battle Between Government and the Marketplace That Is Remaking the Modern World* (New York: Simon & Schuster, 1998) is excellent on the relationship between governments and companies.

An excellent introduction to business in the ancient world is *Foundations of Corporate Empire* by Karl Moore and David Lewis (London: Financial Times/Prentice Hall, 2000). The best starting point for the Middle Ages and Renaissance is Fernand Braudel's monumental *Civilization and Capitalism: 15th–18th Century* (New York: Harper & Row, 1982). Iris Origo's *The Merchant of Prato: Daily Life in a Medieval Italian City* (London: Penguin, 1992) provides a micro-view to complement Braudel's macro.

The most eminent historian of the East India Company is K. N. Chaudhuri; see *The East India Company: The Study of an Early Joint-Stock Company, 1600–1640* (New York: Reprints of Economic Classics, Augustus M. Kelley, Bookseller, 1965) and *The Trading World of Asia and the English East India Company* (Cambridge: Cambridge University Press, 1978). Other useful studies are John Keay's *The Honourable Company: A History of the English East India Company* (New York: Macmillan, 1991) and Philip Lawson's *The East India Company: A History* (London: Longman, 1993). *Nathaniel's Nutmeg: How One Man's Courage Changed the Course of History* (London: Spectre, 1999), by Giles Milton, provides the most entertaining description of the Company's early days.

The most engaging account of the shenanigans of the South Sea Company is a novel written by an American academic: *A Conspiracy of Paper: A Novel* (New York: Ballantine, 2001) by David Liss. A more conventional account is John Carswell's *The South Sea Bubble* (Palo Alto: Stanford University Press, 1960). P.G.M. Dickson's *The Financial Revolution in England: A Study in the Development of Public Credit 1688–1756* (Aldershot, Hampshire, U.K.: Gregg Revivals, 1993 edition) is academic history at its best. The best introduction to the extraordinary John Law is H. Montgomery Hyde's *John Law: The History of an Honest Adventurer* (London: Home & Van Thal, 1948). On the history of financial panics in general, see: Charles Kindelberger's *Manias, Panics and Crashes: A History of Financial Crises* (3d ed., New York: John Wiley, 1996) and Niall Ferguson's *The Cash Nexus: Money and Power in the Modern World 1700–2000* (London: Allen Lane, 2001). Ferguson's two-volume history of the Rothschilds, *The House of Rothschild: Money's Prophets 1798–1848* (New York: Penguin, 1999) and *The House of Rothschild: The World's Banker 1849–1999* (New York: Penguin, 2000), also provides one of the best overviews of European capitalism.

Armand Budington DuBois's *The English Business Company after the Bubble Act 1720–1800* (New York: Octagon Books, 1971) traces the impact of a calamitous piece of legislation. One day a historian will write a great book on the debate about the joint-stock company in nineteenth-century England. Until then, the following books are useful: Charles Kindelberger's *A Financial History of Western Europe* (Oxford: Oxford University Press, 1993), L.C.B. Gower's *The Principles of Modern Company Law* (London: Stevens and Sons, 1954), James Jefferys's *Business Organizations in Great Britain 1856–1914* (New York: Arno Press, 1977), and P. L. Cottrell's *Industrial Finance 1830–1914: The Finance and Organization of English Manufacturing Industry* (London: Methuen, 1980).

The best introduction to the rise of big business in America is, of course, Alfred Chandler. For a contrary view, see William Roy's *Socializing Capital: The Rise of the Large Industrial Corporation in America* (Princeton: Princeton University Press, 1997) and Charles Perrow's *Organizing America: Wealth, Power and the Origins of Corporate Capitalism* (Princeton: Princeton University Press, 2002). A classic short account of society's attempts to adjust to big business is by Samuel P. Hays: *The Response to Industrialism 1885–1914* (Chicago: University of Chicago Press, 1957). Other useful works (chosen almost arbitrarily out of the vast literature on the subject) might include Olivier Zunz's *Making America Corporate, 1870–1920* (Chicago: University of Chicago Press, 1990), Naomi Lamoreauz's *The Great Merger Movement in American Business, 1895–1904* (Cambridge: Cambridge University Press, 1985), and Richard Tedlow's *Giants of Enterprise: Seven Business Innovators and the Empires They Built* (New York: Harper-Business, 2001). Two books by Ron Chernow put human faces on the rise of big business: *Titan: The Life of John D. Rockefeller* (New York: Random House, 1998) and *The House of Morgan: An American Banking Dynasty and the Rise of Modern Finance* (New York: Atlantic Monthly Press, 1990).

Alfred Chandler's *Scale and Scope: The Dynamics of Indus-*

trial Capitalism (Cambridge, Mass.: Harvard University Press, 1990) is also the best introduction to the rise of the company in Britain and Germany. An indispensable source on Britain is Leslie Hannah's *The Rise of the Corporate Economy* (London: Methuen, 1983). Martin J. Wiener's *English Culture and the Decline of the Industrial Spirit* (Cambridge: Cambridge University Press, 1981) lays out some of the reasons why Britain failed to embrace companies. The relevant essays in *Creating Modern Capitalism: How Entrepreneurs, Companies and Counties Triumphed in Three Industrial Revolutions* (Cambridge, Mass.: Harvard University Press), edited by Thomas McCraw, provide introductions to corporate development in Germany and Japan. See also Masahiko Aoki and Ronald Dore's *The Japanese Firm* (New York: Oxford University Press, 1994).

The best source on Alfred Sloan is Alfred Sloan: *My Years with General Motors* (Garden City, N.Y.: Doubleday, 1963), one of the finest management books ever written. Thomas McCraw's *American Business, 1920–2000: How It Worked* (Wheeling, Ill.: Harlan Davidson, 2000) is an excellent introduction. See also his classic *Prophets of Regulation: Charles Francis Adams, Louis Brandeis, James Landis, Alfred Kahn* (Cambridge, Mass.: Belknap Press, 1984).

The sources on the unbundling of the company are voluminous: you could probably find interesting insights by reading any of the business magazines published in this period. A few highlights chosen almost at random: Michael Jensen's 'Eclipse of the Public Cor-poration,' *Harvard Business Review* (September/October 1989); Daniel Jones, James Womack, and Daniel Roos's *The Machine That Changed the World: The Story of Lean Production* (New York: Rawson Associates, 1990); AnnaLee Saxanian's *Regional Advantage: Culture and Competition in Silicon Valley and Route 128* (Cambridge, Mass.:

Harvard University Press, 1994); Marina Whitman's *New World, New Rules: The Changing Role of the American Corporation* (Boston: Harvard Business School Press, 1999); and Nitin Nohria, Davis Dyer, and Frederick Dalzell's *Changing Fortunes: Remaking the Industrial Corporation* (New York: John Wiley, 2002).

The most insightful commentator on multinationals was the late Raymond Vernon. See his *Sovereignty at Bay* (New York: Basic Books, 1977) and *In the Hurricane's Eye: The Troubled Prospects of Multinational Enterprises* (Cambridge, Mass.: Harvard University Press, 1998). Anything by Charles Wilson is also worth devouring (though some of his best writing is buried in obscure academic collections). Mira Wilkins has edited two useful collections of essays on multinationals. She is also the author of a standard book on American multinationals, *The Emergence of Multinational Enterprise* (Cambridge, Mass.: Harvard University Press, 1970). The best introduction to British multinationals is *British Multinationals: Origins, Management and Performance*, edited by Geoffrey Jones (Aldershot, Hampshire, U.K.: Gower, 1986).

Notes

INTRODUCTION: *UTOPIA LIMITED*

1. K. Theodore Hoppen, *The Mid-Victorian Generation, 1846–1886*, New Oxford History of England (Oxford: Clarendon Press, 1998).
2. Quoted in Jack Beatty, ed., *Colossus: How the Corporation Changed America* (New York: Broadway Books, 2001), 18. See also Stephen Innes, *Creating the Commonwealth: The Economic Culture of Puritan New England* (New York: Norton, 1995), 206–9, 212–14.
3. A. V. Dicey, *Law and Opinion in England* (London: Macmillan, 1920), 245.
4. Anthony Trollope, *The Way We Live Now* (New York: Penguin Books, 2002), 78.
5. Thomas McCraw, *American Business 1920–2000: How It Worked* (Wheeling, Ill.: Harlan Davidson, 2000), 47.
6. James Watson, ed., *Golden Arches East: McDonald's in East Asia* (Stanford: Stanford University Press, 1998).
7. This happened among others to Peter Verhoef, the commander of one Dutch East Indies fleet, who was lured into a spot on the island of Neira by the Bandanese, and duly slaughtered with forty of his men.
8. Douglas North and R. P. Thomas, *The Rise of the Western World* (Cambridge: Cambridge University Press, 1973); Nathan Rosenberg and L. E. Birdzell, *How the West Grew Rich: The Economic Transformation of the Industrial World* (New York: Basic Books, 1986).
9. Rosenberg and Birdzell, *How the West Grew Rich*, 190.
10. Ibid., 22–32.
11. In 1998 (the last year for which figures are available), companies accounted for around 90 percent of the sales and receipts reported by American businesses.

ONE: MERCHANTS AND MONOPOLISTS, 3000 B.C.–A.D. 1500

1. Jonathan Barron Baskin and Paul J. Miranti, *A History of Corporate*

Finance (Cambridge: Cambridge University Press, 1997), 29.

2. Quoted in Peter Jay, *Road to Riches* (London: Weidenfeld & Nicolson, 2000), 49.

3. Karl Moore and David Lewis, *Foundations of Corporate Empire* (London: Financial Times/Prentice Hall, 2001), 33.

4. Ibid., 67.

5. Ibid., 97.

6. A.H.M. Jones, *The Roman Economy: Studies in Ancient Economic and Administrative History* (Oxford: Basil Blackwell, 1974).

7. Quoted in Oscar Handlin and Mary Handlin, 'Origins of the American Business Corporation,' in Frederic Lane (ed.), *Enterprise and Secular Change* (Homewood, Ill.: Richard Irwin, 1953).

8. M. Rostovtzeff, *Social and Economic History of the Roman Empire* (Oxford: Oxford University Press, 1926), 160.

9. Richard Duncan-Jones, *The Economy of the Roman Empire: Quantitative Studies* (Cambridge: Cambridge University Press, 1977), 33.

10. Timur Koran, 'The Islamic Commercial Crisis: Institutional Roots of Economic Underdevelopment in the Middle East,' University of Southern California Research Paper, available at http://papers2.ssrn.com/paper.taf?pip_jrnl=276635.

11. Fernand Braudel, *Civilization and Capitalism, 15th–18th Century.* Vol. II: *The Wheels of Commerce* (New York: Harper & Row, 1982), 434.

12. Baskin and Miranti, *A History of Corporate Finance*, 50.

13. Figure quoted in Howard Means, *Money and Power: The History of Business* (New York: John Wiley, 2001), 36.

14. Baskin and Miranti, *A History of Corporate Finance*, 43–44.

15. Most of the information about Datini comes from Iris Origo's excellent *The Merchant of Prato: Daily Life in a Medieval Italian City* (London: Penguin, 1992).

16. Ibid., 81.

17. Quoted in ibid., 110.

18. Braudel, *The Wheels of Commerce*, 437.

19. Eileen Power, *The Wool Trade in English Medieval History* (Oxford: Oxford University Press, 1942, 1955), 96–103.

TWO: IMPERIALISTS AND SPECULATORS, 1500–1750

1. Fernand Braudel, *The Wheels of Commerce*, 440.

2. Jack Beatty, ed., *Colossus: How the Corporation Changed America*, 6.

3. Quoted in Beatty, *Colossus*, 6–8.

4. Quoted in Giles Milton, *Nathaniel's Nutmeg: How One Man's Courage Changed the Course of History* (London: Spectre, 1999), 35.
5. Quoted in ibid., 139.
6. Braudel, *The Wheels of Commerce*, 443.
7. John Keay, *The Honourable Company: A History of the English East India Company* (New York: Macmillan, 1991), xxii.
8. Quoted in Milton, *Nathaniel's Nutmeg*, 91.
9. K. N. Chaudhuri, *The English East India Company: The Study of an Early Joint-Stock Company, 1600–1640* (New York: Reprints of Economic Classics, Augustus M. Kelley, Bookseller, 1965), 208–11.
10. Keay, *The Honourable Company*, 113.
11. Ibid., 113.
12. Chaudhuri, *East India Company*, 111–39.
13. Ibid., 140–72.
14. Baskin and Miranti, *A History of Corporate Finance*, 78.
15. Thomas McCraw, ed., *Creating Modern Capitalism: How Entrepreneurs, Companies and Countries Triumphed in Three Industrial Revolutions* (Cambridge, Mass.: Harvard University Press), 59.
16. Saul David, *The Indian Mutiny 1857* (London: Viking, 2002).
17. Niall Ferguson, *The Cash Nexus: Money and Power in the Modern World 1700–2000* (London: Allen Lane, 2001), 310–15.
18. Quoted in P.G.M. Dickson, *The Financial Revolution in England: A Study in the Development of Public Credit in England 1688–1756* (Aldershot, Hampshire, U.K.: Gregg Revivals, 1993), 84.
19. Ibid., 72.
20. For a readable account of the South Sea Bubble, see David Liss, *A Conspiracy of Paper: A Novel* (New York: Ballantine, 2001).
21. Dickson, *The Financial Revolution in England*, 118.
22. Ibid., 112–14.
23. Ibid., 90.
24. Ferguson, *The Cash Nexus*, 118.
25. Dickson, *The Financial Revolution in England*, 90.
26. Both quoted in Anthony Sampson, *Company Man: The Rise and Fall of Corporate Life* (New York: Times Business, 1995), 17.
27. Quoted in Lawrence James, *Raj: The Making and Unmaking of British India* (London: Abacus, 1998), 49.
28. Beatty, *Colossus*, 18.
29. Stephen Innes, 'From Corporation to Commonwealth,' in ibid., 18.
30. Adam Smith, *An Inquiry into the Nature and Causes of the Wealth of Nations*, vol. 2 (New York: Oxford University Press, 1976), 733. He details the shortcomings of chartered companies on pp. 733–58.

31. K. N. Chaudhuri, *The Trading World of Asia and the English East India Company* (Cambridge: Cambridge University Press, 1978), 454.

32. Ann Carlos and Stephen Nicholas, 'Giants of an Earlier Capitalism: The Chartered Trading Companies as Modern Multinationals,' *Business History Review* 62 (Autumn 1988): 398–419.

33. Keay, *The Honourable Company*, 170.

34. Quoted in Sampson, *Company Man*, 19.

THREE: A PROLONGED AND PAINFUL BIRTH, 1750–1862

1. Paul Langford, *A Polite and Commercial People: England 1727–1783* (Oxford: Oxford University Press, 1989), 396ff.

2. Quoted in William Roy, *Socializing Capital: The Rise of the Large Industrial Corporation in America* (Princeton: Princeton University Press, 1997), 53.

3. Langford, *A Polite and Commercial People*, 396ff.

4. Armand Budington DuBois, *The English Business Company after the Bubble Act 1720–1800* (New York: Octagon Books, 1971).

5. Charles Kindleberger, *A Financial History of Western Europe* (Oxford: Oxford University Press, 1993).

6. Hugh Thomas, *The Slave Trade* (New York: Simon & Schuster, 1997), 225.

7. Ibid., 294.

8. Leslie Hannah, *The Rise of the Corporate Economy* (London: Methuen, 1983), 19.

9. Howard Means, *Money and Power: The History of Business* (New York: John Wiley, 2001), 101.

10. Charles Perrow, *Organizing America: Wealth, Power and the Origins of Corporate Capitalism* (Princeton: Princeton University Press, 2002), 33.

11. Roy, *Socializing Capital*, 49.

12. Handlin and Handlin, 'Origins of the American Business Corporation,' 119–20.

13. Roy, *Socializing Capital*, 46.

14. Ibid., 54.

15. Charles Freedeman, *Joint-Stock Enterprise in France 1807–1867: From Privileged Company to Modern Corporation* (Chapel Hill: University of North Carolina Press, 1979).

16. P. L. Cottrell, *Industrial Finance 1830–1914: The Finance and Organization of English Manufacturing Industry* (London: Methuen, 1980), 42.

17. Ibid., 43.
18. Kindleberger, *A Financial History of Western Europe*, 195.
19. Baskin and Miranti, *A History of Corporate Finance*, 136.
20. Ibid., 152.
21. Ruth Dudley Edwards, *The Pursuit of Reason* (London: Hamish Hamilton, 1993), 90.
22. L.C.B. Gower, *The Principles of Modern Company Law* (London: Stevens and Sons, 1954), 41–42.
23. James Jefferys, *Business Organization in Great Britain 1856–1914* (New York: Arno Press, 1977), 20–21.
24. Ibid., 41.
25. Quoted in Andrew Gamble and Gavin Kelly, 'The Politics of the Company,' in John Parkinson, Andrew Gamble, and Gavin Kelly, *The Political Economy of the Company* (Oxford: Hart, 2000), 32.
26. Freedeman, *Joint-Stock Enterprise in France 1807–1867*, 132–33.
27. We are indebted to Dr. Simon Green of All Souls College for this insight.
28. Robert Lowe's speech on March 13, 1866, in G. M. Young and W. D. Handcock, eds., *English Historical Documents 1833–1874*, vol. 12, part 1 (New York: Oxford University Press, 1956), 165.
29. Gower, *The Principles of Modern Company Law*, 48.
30. Nicholas Crafts, 'Institutional Quality and European Development Before and After the Industrial Revolution,' paper for the World Bank, Washington, D.C., July 2000.
31. We are grateful to Leslie Hannah for this observation.
32. Quoted in Cottrell, *Industrial Finance 1830–1914*, 58.
33. Cottrell, *Industrial Finance 1830–1914*, 55.
34. See Gamble and Kelly, 'The Politics of the Company.'
35. Quoted in Sampson, *Company Man*, 26.

FOUR: THE RISE OF BIG BUSINESS IN AMERICA, 1862–1913

1. Quoted in Alfred Chandler, *Scale and Scope: The Dynamics of Industrial Capitalism* (Cambridge, Mass.: Harvard University Press, 1990), 61.
2. Alfred Chandler, *The Visible Hand: The Managerial Revolution in American Business* (Cambridge, Mass.: Harvard University Press, 1977), 17.
3. Michael Leapman, *The World for a Shilling: How the Great Exhibition of 1851 Shaped a Nation* (London: Headline, 2001), 129.
4. Chandler, *Scale and Scope*, 47.
5. Richard Tedlow, *Giants of Enterprise: Seven Business Innovators*

and the Empires They Built (New York: HarperBusiness, 2001), 66.

6. See Chandler, *The Visible Hand*, 80–144.

7. Chandler, *Scale and Scope*, 53.

8. Chandler, *The Visible Hand*, 92.

9. Charles R. Geisst, *Wall Street: A History* (New York: Oxford University Press, 1997), 70.

10. Roy, *Socializing Capital*, 108.

11. Baskin and Miranti, *A History of Corporate Finance*, 150.

12. Chandler, *The Visible Hand*, 204–5.

13. See ibid., 209–39.

14. John Micklethwait and Adrian Wooldridge, *A Future Perfect* (London: Random House Business, 2001).

15. Quoted in Tedlow, *Giants of Enterprise*, 58.

16. Chandler, *The Visible Hand*, 280.

17. See ibid., 285–379.

18. Ron Chernow, *Titan: The Life of John D. Rockefeller, Sr.* (New York: Random House, 1998), 150–51.

19. Ibid., 332.

20. Ibid., 430.

21. Jonathan Rowe, 'Reinventing the Corporation,' *Washington Monthly* (April, 1996).

22. Tedlow, *Giants of Enterprise*, 59.

23. Thomas McCraw, 'American Capitalism,' in McCraw, ed., *Creating Modern Capitalism*, 320.

24. Tedlow, *Giants of Enterprise*, 421–22.

25. Baskin and Miranti, *A History of Corporate Finance*, 178–79.

26. James P. Young, *Reconsidering American Liberalism: The Troubled Odyssey of the Liberal Idea* (Boulder: Westview, 1996), 130.

27. Sampson, *Company Man*, 27.

28. Geisst, *Wall Street*, 131.

29. Samuel P. Hays, *The Response to Industrialism 1885–1914* (Chicago: University of Chicago Press, 1957), 54.

30. Roland Marchand, *Creating the Corporate Soul: The Rise of Public Relations and Corporate Imagery in American Big Business* (Berkeley: University of California Press, 1998), 1–87.

31. E. Digby Baltzell, *An American Business Aristocracy* (New York: Free Press, 1962), 135.

32. Ibid., 120.

33. Tedlow, *Giants of Enterprise*, 104.

FIVE: THE RISE OF BIG BUSINESS IN BRITAIN, GERMANY, AND JAPAN, 1850–1950

1. Hannah, *The Rise of the Corporate Economy*, 17.
2. Ibid., 1.
3. Chandler, *Scale and Scope*, 313.
4. George Orwell, *The Road to Wigan Pier* (Harmondsworth, U.K.: Penguin, 1962), 140.
5. Martin J. Wiener, *English Culture and the Decline of the Industrial Spirit, 1850–1980* (Cambridge: Cambridge University Press, 1981), 131.
6. Quoted in Neil McKendrick, 'General Introduction' to R. J. Overy, *William Morris, Viscount Nuffield* (London: Europa Publications, 1976), xl.
7. J. B. Priestley, *English Journey* (London: Heinemann, 1934), 64.
8. Michael Sanderson, *The Universities and British Industry, 1850–1970* (London: Routledge and Kegan Paul, 1972), 282–83.
9. Gordon Roderick and Michael Stephens, 'The British Educational System,' in Gordon Roderick and Michael Stephens, eds., *The British Malaise: Industrial Performance, Education and Training in Britain Today* (Barcombe, Sussex, U.K.: Falmer Press, 1982).
10. Sanderson, *Universities and British Industry*, 282–83.
11. Quoted in Sampson, *Company Man*, 59.
12. Leslie Hannah, 'Marshall's Trees and the Global Forest: Were Giant Redwoods Different?,' in Naomi Lamoreaux, Daniel Raff, and Peter Tremin, eds., *Markets, Firms and Countries* (Chicago: University of Chicago Press, 1999), 265.
13. Leslie Hannah, 'The American Miracle, 1875–1950 and After: A View in the American Mirror,' *Business and Economic History* 24, no. 2 (Winter 1994).
14. Charles Wilson, 'Multinationals, Management and World Markets: A Historical View,' in Harold Williamson, ed., *Evolution of International Management Structures* (Newark, Del.: University of Delaware Press, 1975), 209.
15. McCraw, *American Business 1920–2000*, 48.
16. Chandler, *Scale and Scope*, 423.
17. Jeffrey Frear, 'German Capitalism,' in McCraw, ed., *Creating Modern Capitalism*, 142–43.
18. Ibid., 165.
19. A. E. Twentyman, 'Note on the Earlier History of the Technical High Schools in Germany,' Board of Education, *Special Report on Educational Subjects*. Vol. 9: *Education in Germany* (London: His Majesty's Stationery Office, 1902), 465.

20. Peter Drucker, *Post-Capitalist Society* (London: Butterworth Heinemann, 1993), 33.
21. R. B. Haldane, 'Great Britain and Germany: A Study in Education,' in *Education and Empire: Addresses on Certain Topics of the Day* (London, 1902), 28.
22. Frear, 'German Capitalism,' 140.
23. Ibid., 145–46.
24. Chandler, *Scale and Scope*, 500.
25. Frear, 'German Capitalism,' 144.
26. Jeffrey Bernstein, 'Japanese Capitalism,' in McCraw, ed., *Creating Modern Capitalism*, 447–48.
27. Francis Fukuyama, *Trust: The Social Virtues and the Creation of Prosperity* (London: Penguin, 1996), 162.
28. Sampson, *Company Man*, 33.
29. Bernstein, 'Japanese Capitalism,' 460.
30. Moore and Lewis, *Foundations of Corporate Empire*, 248.

SIX: THE TRIUMPH OF MANAGERIAL CAPITALISM, 1913–1975

1. Hannah, 'Marshall's Trees and the Global Forest,' 58.
2. Baltzell, *An American Business Aristocracy*, 449.
3. Alfred Sloan, *My Years with General Motors* (Garden City, N.Y.: Doubleday, 1963).
4. Tedlow, *Giants of Enterprise*, 171.
5. John Byrne, *The Whiz Kids: Ten Founding Fathers of American Business – and the Legacy They Left Us* (New York: Doubleday Currency, 1993), 106.
6. Tedlow, *Giants of Enterprise*, 174.
7. Chandler, *Scale and Scope*, 207.
8. McCraw, *American Business 1920–2000*, 24.
9. Chandler, *Scale and Scope*, 177.
10. McCraw, *American Business 1920–2000*, 48.
11. Sampson, *Company Man*, 41.
12. Ibid., 71–73.
13. Quoted in Milton, *Nathaniel's Nutmeg*, 137.
14. Peter Drucker, *The Concept of the Corporation* (New York: Mentor, 1983), 78.
15. Ibid., 132.
16. Robert Averitt, *The Dual Economy: The Dynamics of American Industry Structure* (New York: Norton, 1968).
17. Chandler, *Scale and Scope*, 609.
18. Baskin and Miranti, *A History of Corporate Finance*, 242.

19. Robert Reich, *The Future of Success* (New York: Knopf, 2001), 71.
20. Company Man's best biographer is Anthony Sampson, though he would not claim to have invented the phrase; Organization Man was the creation of William H. Whyte.

SEVEN: THE CORPORATE PARADOX, 1975–2002

1. Daniel Yergin and Joseph Stanislaw, *The Commanding Heights: The Battle Between Government and the Marketplace That Is Remaking the Modern World* (New York: Simon & Schuster, 1998), 60–64.
2. Ibid., 114.
3. Ibid., 285–89.
4. Nitin Nohria, Davis Dyer, and Frederick Dalzell, *Changing Fortunes: Remaking the Industrial Corporation* (New York: John Wiley, 2002), 4.
5. Ibid., 24.
6. Tom Stewart, *The Wealth of Knowledge* (London: Nicholas Brealey, 2002), 8.
7. George Baker and Thomas Hubbard, 'Make versus Buy in Trucking,' Harvard Business School Working Paper.
8. Fernando Flores and John Gray, *Entrepreneurship and the Wired Life* (London: Demos, 2000), 13.
9. 'Special Report: Car Manufacturing,' *Economist*, February 23, 2002.
10. Bill Emmott, *Japanophobia: The Myth of the Invincible Japanese* (New York: Times Books, 1992), 25.
11. Ibid., 41.
12. Michael Porter, Hirotaka Takeuchi, and Mariko Sakakibara, *Can Japan Compete?* (London: Macmillan, 2000), 69.
13. Ibid., 77.
14. Nohria, Dyer, and Dalzell, *Changing Fortunes*, 187.
15. Bennett Stewart and David Glassman, quoted in Michael Jensen, 'The Eclipse of the Public Corporation,' *Harvard Business Review* (October 1989).
16. George P. Baker and George David Smith, *The New Financial Capitalists: Kohlberg Kravis Roberts and the Creation of Corporate Value* (Cambridge: Cambridge University Press, 1998).
17. Susan Faludi, 'Reckoning at Safeway,' in Beatty, ed., *Colossus*, 406.
18. Baskin and Miranti, *A History of Corporate Finance*, 295.
19. Robert Monks, *The New Global Investors* (Oxford: Capstone, 2001), 69.
20. The classic account of this is AnnaLee Saxenian, *Regional Advantage: Culture and Competition in Silicon Valley and Route 128*

(Cambridge, Mass.: Harvard University Press, 1994).

21. Joint Venture Silicon Valley, 2002 Index, see: http://www.joint-venture.org/resources/2002Index/index.html.

22. Frances Cairncross, *The Company of the Future* (Boston: Harvard Business School Press, 2002), 4.

23. Tedlow, *Giants of Enterprise*, 385.

24. John Byrne, *Chainsaw: The Notorious Career of Al Dunlap in the Era of Profit-at-Any-Price* (New York: HarperBusiness, 1999), 27.

25. Nicholas Lemann, 'Letter from Philadelphia,' *New Yorker*, June 5, 2000.

26. Quoted in Sampson, *Company Man*, 217.

27. Nicholas Varchaver, 'Who's the King of Delaware?,' *Fortune*, May 13, 2002.

28. In 1983, Americans who were between twenty-five and thirty-four had spent a median 3 years with the same employer; by 1996, the figure was 2.8 years. In the thirty-five to forty-four age group, the figure actually rose from 5.2 years in 1983 to 5.3 in 1996, though the figures fell again for older age groups, with the median tenure for the fifty-five to sixty-four age group dropping from 12.2 years to 10.2 years.

29. Stewart, *The Wealth of Knowledge*, 27.

30. http://www.britishchambers.org.uk/cutredtape/burdensbarometer2.htm.

31. Thomas Hopkins, of the Rochester Institute of Technology.

32. Gerald Seib and John Harwood, 'Rising Anxiety: What Could Bring 1930s-Style Reform of U.S. Businesses,' *Wall Street Journal*, July 25, 2002.

33. Quoted in David Leonhardt, 'The Imperial Chief Executive Is Suddenly in the Cross Hairs,' *New York Times*, June 24, 2002.

34. Daniel Kadlec, 'WorldCon,' *Time*, July 8, 2002.

EIGHT: AGENTS OF INFLUENCE: MULTINATIONALS, 1850–2002

1. Charles Wilson, 'The Multinational in Historical Perspective' in K. Nakagawa, ed., *Strategy and Structure in Big Business* (Tokyo, 1974), 270.

2. Ibid., 271.

3. Ibid., 274.

4. Geoffrey Jones, ed., *British Multinationals: Origins, Management and Performance* (Aldershot, Hampshire, U.K.: Gower, 1986), 4.

5. Ibid., 4.

6. Ibid., 7.

7. The phrase 'free-standing companies' was coined by Mira Wilkins. See Mira Wilkins, 'European and North American Multinationals, 1870–1914: Comparisons and Contrasts,' *Business History* 30 (1988): 15–16.

8. Jones, *British Multinationals*, 13.

9. Wilkins, 'European and North American Multinationals,' 21.

10. Ibid., 25.

11. Ibid., 27–28.

12. Mira Wilkins, 'Japanese Multinationals,' *Business History Review* 60 (1986): 207.

13. Ibid., 209.

14. Ibid., 218.

15. Ibid., 221.

16. Ibid., 222.

17. Chandler, *The Visible Hand*, 369.

18. Chandler, *Scale and Scope*, 200.

19. Jones, *British Multinationals*, 5.

20. Sampson, *Company Man*, 143.

21. Paul Doremus et al., *The Myth of the Global Corporation* (Princeton: Princeton University Press, 1998), 8.

22. Quoted in Yves Doz et al., *From Global to Metanational: How Companies Win in the Knowledge Economy* (Boston: Harvard Business School Press, 2001), 63.

23. Peter Drucker, *The New Realities* (London: Heinemann, 1989), 119.

24. Doz et al., *From Global to Metanational*, 13.

25. These statistics all come from 'How Big Are Multinational Companies?,' a paper released in January 2002 by Paul de Grauwe, of the University of Leuven, and Filip Camerman, of the Belgian Senate.

26. Quoted in Langford, *A Polite and Commercial People*, 534.

27. The Casement Report can be found online at: http://web.jjay.cuny.edu/~jobrien/reference/ob73.html.

28. Clive Crook, 'A Survey of Globalisation,' *Economist*, Septem-ber 27, 2001, 15.

29. Wilson, 'The Multinational in Historical Perspective,' 297.

Conclusion: The Future of the Company

1. Woodrow Wilson, *The New Freedom* (New York: Doubleday, 1913).

2. This is a phrase borrowed from Leslie Hannah.

3. Fariborz Ghadar and Pankaj Ghemawat, 'The Dubious Logic of Global Megamergers,' *Harvard Business Review* 78, no. 4 (July–August 2000).

4. Reich, *The Future of Success,* 84–85.
5. See Reinier Kraakman, 'The Durability of the Corporate Form,' in Paul DiMaggio, ed., *The Twenty-first Century Firm: Changing Economic Organization in International Perspective* (Princeton: Princeton University Press, 2001), 147–60.
6. Leslie Hannah, 'The Moral Economy of Business: A Historical Perspective on Ethics and Efficiency,' in Paul Burke, Brian Harrison, and Paul Slack, eds., *Civil Histories: Essays Presented to Sir Keith Thomas* (Oxford: Oxford University Press, 2000).

Quotation from 'A Cooking Egg' from *Collected Poems, 1909–1962* by T. S. Eliot (London: Faber and Faber).

Index